Klasse vorbereitet

Klassenarbeitstrainer

Englisch

Realschule
Gesamtschule
7

W0336578

Schroedel

Klasse vorbereitet

Klassenarbeitstrainer

Englisch
Realschule
Gesamtschule 7

Marcus Lachmund
sowie Clare Fielder und Christine Stakenborg

Marcus Lachmund unterrichtet Englisch und Geschichte an der Realschule. Er ist Seminarlehrer für Englisch und Lehrbeauftragter an einer Universität.

Druck [1]/Jahr 2012

Redaktion: imprint, Zusmarshausen
Kontakt: lernhilfen@schroedel.de
Herstellung: Sandra Grünberg
Umschlaggestaltung und Innenlayout: Maike Frach, Braunschweig
Umschlagfoto: Peter Wirtz, Dormagen
Illustrationen: Thies Schwarz, Hannover
Sprachaufnahmen: Tonstudio Flödl, Ziemetshausen
Satz: imprint, Zusmarshausen
Druck und Bindung: westermann druck GmbH, Braunschweig

ISBN 978-3-507-**23265**-5

Vorwort

Liebe Schülerin, lieber Schüler,

mit diesem Buch gelangst du in drei Schritten zur erfolgreichen Klassenarbeit:

Verstehen: Lerne und wiederhole wichtige **Regeln**. Ausführliche Beispiele und Erklärungen erleichtern dir das Verstehen.

Üben: Abwechslungsreiche **Tests** üben den Lernstoff ein. Wenn du dir einmal nicht sicher bist, wie eine Aufgabe gelöst wird, schaue in den Regeln nach.

Können: Genug geübt? Dann schreibe eine **Klassenarbeit** wie in der Schule! Die Zeitangabe auf jeder Klassenarbeit gibt an, wie viel Zeit dir zur Verfügung steht.

Mithilfe des **Lösungsteils** hinten im Buch kannst du kontrollieren, ob du alle Aufgaben richtig bearbeitet hast.
Hier findest du auch den Bewertungsschlüssel für die Klassenarbeiten.

Zwei Symbole begleiten dich durch das Buch: Der Smiley macht dich auf Tipps und Tricks aufmerksam, das Ausrufezeichen kennzeichnet Aufgaben, die etwas kniffliger sind.

Solltest du einmal nicht genug Platz zum Bearbeiten der Aufgaben finden, nimm einfach ein Heft zur Hand.

Viel Erfolg bei der nächsten Klassenarbeit!

Marcus Lachmund

Inhaltsverzeichnis

verstehen

1 Present tense/past tense

Simple present/present progressive

Für das deutsche Präsens – die Gegenwart – gibt es im Englischen **zwei Zeitformen**:
- das *simple present* und
- das *present progressive.*

Der Satz „Tom spielt Fußball." kann zweierlei bedeuten:
1. John spielt regelmäßig Fußball (im Verein, als Hobby etc.).
2. John spielt jetzt gerade (im Augenblick) Fußball.

Im Englischen muss man für Satz 1 das ***simple present*** verwenden *("John plays football.")* und für Satz 2 das ***present progressive*** *("John is playing football.")*.

Simple present

Bildung des *simple present*
infinitive *(Grundform des Verbs)* + **s** *bei he, she, it*
*We **drink** tea. John **reads** books.*

Grundregel:
He, she, it – s muss mit!

Im *simple present* entsprechen alle Formen der Grundform des Verbs. – Einzige Ausnahme sind die Personen *he, she* und *it* (3. Person Singular).

Sonderfall Verneinung und Frage
Bildung der Verneinung:
don't *(= do not)/**doesn't** (= does not bei he, she, it) +* ***infinitive***
*We **don't drink** tea. John **doesn't read** books.*
Bildung der Frage:
do/does *(bei he, she, it) + Subjekt +* ***infinitive***
*Do you **drink** tea? **Does** John **read** books.*

Für Verneinung und Frage im *simple present* brauchen wir das **Hilfsverb *to do***. Bei *he, she* und *it* verwenden wir ***doesn't*** (Verneinung) und ***does*** (Frage), bei allen anderen Personen verwenden wir ***don't*** (Verneinung) und ***do*** (Frage).

Verwendung des *simple present*

Das *simple present* wird verwendet, wenn etwas regelmäßig (1), immer (2), normalerweise (3), oft oder nie (4) passiert.

(1) *Every morning Tom drinks a glass of milk.*
(2) *John always works hard.*
(3) *We usually come home at six o'clock.*
(4) *Jane often eats fish but she never eats meat.*

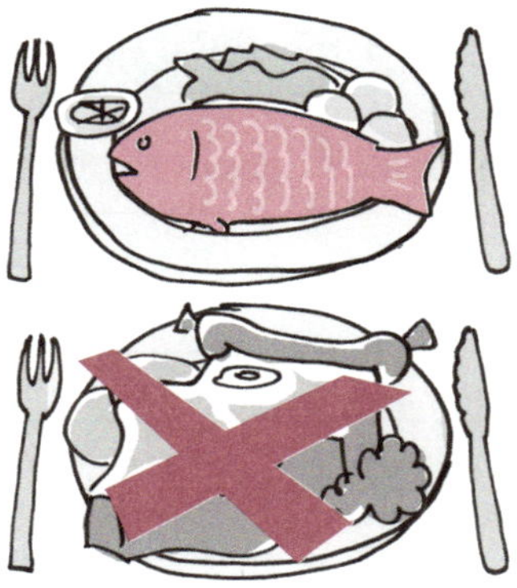

Present progressive

Bildung des *present progressive*

Form von ***to be*** + ***infinitive*** + *ing*

They're *(= are)* ***work****ing hard.* ***I'm*** *(= am)* ***sing****ing a song.*

Das *present progressive* besteht aus einer Form von ***to be*** im ***simple present*** *(am, is, are)* und der **Grundform des Verbs,** an die die Endung ***-ing*** angehängt wird.

Verneinung und Frage

Da die Zeitform mit einem Hilfsverb (*to be*) gebildet wird, kann dieses für die Verneinung *(am not, isn't, aren't)* und auch für die Fragestellung benutzt werden.

Bildung der Verneinung:

They aren't working hard. I am not singing a song.

Bildung der Frage:

Are they working hard? Am I singing a song?

Verwendung des *present progressive*

Das *present progressive* wird verwendet, wenn etwas gerade im Augenblick des Sprechens passiert (1) oder eine Handlung gerade (im Augenblick) abläuft (2).

(1) *Look, the boys are running very fast.*
(2) *At the moment Tom and Jane are washing their dad's car.*

Besonderheiten bei der Bildung der *ing*-Form

Bei einigen Verben musst du Besonderheiten bei der Schreibweise der *ing*-Form beachten:

– Endet der Infinitiv auf ein stummes *-e*, fällt dieses bei der *ing*-Form weg.
  drive *– driving,* ***dance*** *– dancing*
  Ganz selten sind zwei Schreibweisen möglich:
  glue (leimen, kleben) – *gluing/glueing*

- Nach einem einzelnen, betonten Vokal wird ein einzelner Endkonsonant verdoppelt.
  *swi**m** – swi**mm**ing, ru**n** – ru**nn**ing*
- Endet das Verb auf *-ie*, wird das *-ie* zu *-y* geändert.
  *l**ie** – l**y**ing, d**ie** – d**y**ing*

Weitere Beispiele für besondere *ing*-Formate:

ride	*riding*	*bake*	*baking*
come	*coming*	*define*	*defining*
hope	*hoping*	*confer*	*conferring*
argue	*arguing*	*describe*	*describing*
beg	*begging*	*stop*	*stopping*
rob	*robbing*	*regret*	*regretting*

Simple past

Bildung des *simple past*

(1) Regelmäßige Verben:
infinitive (Grundform des Verbs) + ***ed***

(2) Unregelmäßige Verben: ***2nd form***

*(1) I **repaired** my car two hours ago.*
*(2) Yesterday we **went** to the cinema.*

Im *simple past* unterscheiden wir bei der Bildung zwischen **regelmäßigen** und **unregelmäßigen Verben**.

- Regelmäßige Verben bilden wir mit der Grundform des Verbs und der Endung *-ed*.
- Unregelmäßige Verben haben Sonderformen, die man auswendig lernen muss. In deinem Schulbuch findest du eine Liste der unregelmäßigen Verben, bestehend aus drei Formen (z. B. *to go, went, gone*). Die zweite Form ist immer die *simple-past*-Form (z. B. *went*).
- In beiden Fällen gibt es für alle Personen (*I, you, he* etc.) nur eine Form.

Sonderfall Verneinung und Frage

Bildung der Verneinung:
didn't** (= did not) + **infinitive
*They **didn't go** to the disco last night.*
*Jack **didn't buy** a CD yesterday.*

Bildung der Frage:
did** + Subjekt + **infinitive
***Did** you **see** the film?*
***Did** Sarah **do** her homework last week?*

Für Verneinung und Frage im *simple past* brauchen wir – wie im *simple present* – das Hilfsverb *to do*, allerdings in seiner Vergangenheitsform ***did***. Bei der Verneinung verwenden wir ***didn't*** und bei der Frage ***did***.

Verwendung des *simple past*
Das *simple past* wird verwendet, um auszudrücken, wann etwas in der **Vergangenheit geschehen ist.** Der Vorgang bzw. die Handlung ist bereits **abgeschlossen**.

Past progressive

Bildung des *past progressive*
was/were *+* ***infinitive*** *+ ing*
Last Saturday afternoon they ***were play****ing tennis.*
I ***was sing****ing a song when the telephone rang.*

Das *past progressive* besteht aus einer Form von ***to be*** im *simple past (was/were)* und der **Grundform des Verbs**, an welches die Endung ***-ing*** angehängt wird.

Verneinung und Frage
Da die Zeitform mit einem **Hilfsverb** ***(to be)*** gebildet wird, kann dieses für die Verneinung ***(wasn't/weren't)*** und auch für die Fragestellung benutzt werden.
Bildung der Verneinung:
They ***weren't*** *(= were not)* ***train****ing yesterday morning.*
I ***wasn't*** *(= was not)* ***driv****ing home last night.*
Bildung der Frage:
Were *you* ***work****ing when they came home?*
Was *she* ***listen****ing when her teacher called her name?*

Ausnahmen
Verben, die **Zustände** (1) oder **Sinneswahrnehmungen** (2) ausdrücken, stehen **nie im *progressive***.
(1) z. B.: *to belong* (gehören), *to contain* (beinhalten), *to know* (wissen), *to love* (lieben), *to like* (mögen), *to need* (brauchen)
(2) z. B.: *to see* (sehen), *to smell* (riechen), *to hear* (hören)

Verwendung des *past progressive*
Das *past progressive* wird verwendet, wenn etwas zu einem bestimmten Zeitpunkt in der Vergangenheit gerade geschah (1), eine Handlung in der Vergangenheit im Verlauf war, als eine andere Handlung einsetzte (2), oder wenn die Dauer einer Tätigkeit in der Vergangenheit betont werden soll (3).
(1) *Yesterday evening I was reading the newspaper.*
(2) *We were playing basketball when it began to rain.*
(3) *She was playing computer games all day long.*

Test 1: *Simple present/present progressive*

üben

1 **Complete the following sentences. Put the verbs in brackets into the *simple present*.**

Every Wednesday John and Jill drive (drive) to London to go shopping. They don't want (not want) to use the bus because it is (be) always very crowded. Sometimes John's little brother Tom goes (go) with them. He doesn't have (not have) much pocket money so he only wants (want) to have some fun in the big city. All three of them love (love) the many famous sights and always try (try) to visit at least one.

2 **Paul is a new pupil. Ask him the following questions in English. Use the *simple present*.**

Du willst wissen,		Die Frage auf Englisch lautet:
a)	wo Paul herkommt.	Where do you come from, Paul?
b)	wo er wohnt.	Where do you live?
c)	welche Fächer er mag.	Which subjects do you like?
d)	welche Hobbys er hat.	Which hobbies do you have?
e)	ob er einen Bruder oder eine Schwester hat.	Do you have a brother or a sister?

3 **Write down the *-ing*-form of the following verbs.**

a) sit ______________________

b) wait ______________________

c) walk ______________________

d) hope ______________________

e) put ______________________

f) try ______________________

üben

4 **Translate into English.**

a) Ich spiele gerade in meinem Zimmer. ______________________________

____

b) Die Schüler hören gerade nicht zu. ______________________________

____

c) Spielen sie gerade Fußball? ______________________________

____

d) Jane macht gerade die Betten. ______________________________

____

e) Im Augenblick spricht er mit Sarah. ______________________________

____

5 **Complete the following dialogue.**
Use either *simple present* or *present progressive*.

Tom: "Hi, Linda. This is Tom. What ____________________ (you, do) at the moment? "

Linda: "I ____________________ (watch) Star Wars – Episode V.
I ____________________ (love) it.
I ____________________ (think) it´s the best Star Wars film."

Tom: "Oh, yes. I ____________________ (like) it, too. Would you like to go swimmming after the film?"

Linda: "That ____________________ (sound) great, but Sarah is also here and she ____________________ (not like) swimming very much. But why ____________________ you ____________________ (not come) and ____________________ (watch) Star Wars with us?"

Tom: "Well, the problem ____________________ (be) that I ____________________ (tidy up) my room at the moment. I always ____________________ (must, tidy up) my room on Mondays."

üben

Linda: "Ok, you ______________________ (can, come) later and we ______________________. ______________________ (want, watch) Episode VI as well."

Tom: "Hm, Episode VI ______________________ (not be) my favourite Star Wars film ..."

Linda: "Oh, Jane ______________________ (come) home now. Maybe she ______________________ (want) to go swimming with you? Wait a moment ..."

Tom: "Ok. And ______________________ she ______________________ (want, go)?"

Jane: "Hi, Tom. Swimming ______________________ (be) great. Let´s meet at the swimming pool in about 30 minutes."

Tom: "Great, see you there."

Test 2: *Simple present/present progressive*

üben

1 **Complete the following questions and answers with a suitable verb from the list. Use either the *simple present* or the *present progressive*.**

do ▪ go ▪ leave ▪ listen ▪ read ▪ try ▪ watch

a) ____________ John ____________ TV? No, he isn't ____________.

He ____________ comics. He never ____________ TV before eight o'clock.

b) ____________ you ____________ your homework?

Yes, ____________. I always ____________ my homework after school.

c) Where ____________ Dave ____________? He ____________ to the cinema. He ____________ every Thursday.

d) Why ____________ you ____________ so early? I usually ____________ to catch the last train home.

e) ____________ the pupils ____________ to their teacher at the moment? Yes, of course. They always ____________ carefully.

2 **Write a letter (about 80 words) to your penfriend in the USA. Tell him about your hobbies, your daily routine and what you are doing at the moment. Use the *simple present* and the *present progressive* as often as possible.**

Dear ____________ ,

____

____

____

____

____

____

____

____

____

Test 3: *Simple past/past progressive*

üben

1 **Complete the sentences with the *simple past form* of the verbs in brackets.**

I went (go) to the cinema yesterday. Two of my friends came (come) with me. We went (go) into town by bike. I wore (wear) a helmet, but one of my friends didn't (do not). I knew (know) it was (be) a long film, so I took (take) my bike lights with me, too. Again, one of my friends' bikes had (have) no lights. When we arrived (arrive) at the cinema, we looked (look) at the posters first. Yes, there they were (be): The posters said (say) the cinema was still showing the film.
We bought (buy) the tickets and ran (run) inside quickly.
Yes, we caught (catch) the best seats in the middle!
We enjoyed (enjoy) the film very much. When we rode (ride) home on our bikes it was (be) already dark. I put (put) on my lights and my helmet, which my friends made (make) a lot of jokes about. I became (become) angry and rode (ride) my bike as fast as I could (can). But then! My friend Nick wanted to have (want to have) some more fun. Toward a sharp bend he overtook (overtake) my bike and then he braked (brake) suddenly in front of me. Of course I crashed (crash) into him. I shouted at (shout at) him angrily before I fell off (fall off) my bike into the mud. My head hit (hit) the ground hard, but luckily I had (have) my helmet on, which protected (protect) me.
My friends never told (tell) jokes about my *silly hat* again.

2 **Make questions to ask for the underlined part of the answer.**

a) Yesterday we went to the cinema.

____

b) Two of my friends went with me.

____

c) We went into town by bike.

____

üben

d) First we looked at the posters.

____

e) We ran inside quickly because we wanted the best seats.

____

____

f) Yes, we enjoyed the film very much.

____

3 Complete the sentences with the *past progressive-form* of the verbs in brackets.

a) Our teacher Mr Miller wanted to know what the pupils (do) __________ last Saturday.

b) Robby said he (practise) __________ the guitar all day.

c) Anna said she (visit) __________ her grandparents in Wales.

d) John and Jack answered they (cycle) __________ to Bradford.

e) David said he (paint) __________ his room.

f) Elizabeth said she (move) __________ house.

g) Diana reported she (run) __________ her first marathon.

4 Complete the dialogue.

Mr Miller: „What __________ (you, do) last Saturday, Robby?"

Robby: „I __________ (play) the guitar."

Mr Miller: „ __________ (you, play) the guitar, too, Anna?"

Anna: „No, I __________ . I __________ (visit) my grandparents. We __________ to their local cinema because they __________ (want, see) the new Bond movie."

Mr Miller: „Oh, really? __________ (you, like) it?"

Anna: „Yes, it __________ (be) great. My grandparents __________ (love) it, too."

5 **Complete the following text. Use either *simple past* or *past progressive*.**

A trip to NYC

Last August, the Millers ________________ (fly) to New York. When they ________________ (arrive) at JFK it ________________ (rain) heavily. Fortunately they ________________ (can, find) a taxi which ________________ (bring) them to their hotel.

The following morning the weather ________________ (be) great again and the sun ________________ (shine). So they ________________ (take) a ferry to Liberty Island because John ________________ ________________ (want, see) the Statue of Liberty. The trip was fantastic and they ________________ (have) a wonderful view of the Manhattan skyline. But John's sister Sally is more into shopping, so they ________________ (walk) down Fifth Avenue in the afternoon. Of course she ________________ (not buy) anything because it´s one of the world´s most expensive places. While Sally and her mother ________________ (look for) extravagant clothing stores like Prada, John and his dad ________________ (go) to the famous toy store FOA Schwartz.

On their second day the Millers ________________ (visit) some very interesting museums and ________________ (have) a picknick at Central Park. The following days they often ________________ (use) the New York Subway and ________________ (see) many other famous sights like the Brooklyn Bridge, Wall Street or Grand Central Station. Of course they also ________________ (go up) the Empire State Building.

They ________________ (must, wait) more than an hour but it ____________ (be) worth it. While they ________________ (look) at all the skyscrapers from above, the sun ________________ (go down) and ________________ (bath) the whole scenery in a wonderful red light. That surely ________________ (be) one of the greatest moments of their trip.

1 **Complete the sentences with the correct form of the verbs in brackets.**

Last week Paul ________________ (go) on a school trip to Stonehenge. The pupils ________________ (sleep) in tents and in the evening they ________________ (make) a big fire, ________________ (sit) around it and ________________ (sing) songs. Then some boys ________________ (want) to listen to scary stories, so they ________________ (ask) their teacher to tell one. Mr Miller ________________ (think) for a while and then he ________________ (tell) this old story:

Many years ago there ________________ (be) two poor old people and their only son. The boy ________________ (be) always hungry and he ________________ (eat) all the time. So he ________________ (grow) fatter and fatter. Because he ________________ (need) so much food and also new clothes every month, his parents ________________ (get) poorer and poorer. One night he ________________ (look) at the moon. It always ________________ (grow) and then ________________ (decrease) in size again and then it all ________________ (start) again from the beginning. He then very much ________________ (wish) to be like the moon, so he ________________ (can) grow fat without having to buy new clothes all the time. In the morning he was gone, but the next night two fat full moons ________________ (shine) among the stars.

Of course, the boys ________________ (not believe) a word of this and they all ________________ (go) to sleep inside their tents.

/24

2 **A Letter to Debbie: Fill in the correct form of the verbs given. Mind the tenses.**

Dear Debbie,

How are you? I ________________ (have) a great time at the moment because my parents ________________ (go) on holiday last Saturday and I ________________ (stay) at my aunt's house for the next two weeks. We ________________ (do) a lot of fun things last weekend, and we ________________ (laugh) at my uncle's jokes all the time. Last

können

Monday I ________________ (tell) my aunt about Alton Towers.

She ________________ (want) to know everything about the attractions

and then we ________________ (go) there last Tuesday.

It ________________ (be) fantastic! On Wednesday I ________________

(try) to phone you but you ________________ (not/be) at home.

I ________________ (want, ask) you about next weekend because I

________________ (want, visit) you over the weekend.

What ________________ (be) your plans? We ________________

(have) a great time together last time!

Please ________________ (phone) me soon!

From Sita

/16

3 **Use your own ideas to complete the sentences.**
Use the *past progressive*.

a) John came home while we

____

b) The doorbell rang while Jane

____

c) They saw an accident while they

____

d) I heard a strange noise while I

____

/4

4 **Put the verbs in brackets into the correct form.**
Use either *simple past* or *past progressive*.

a) Tom ________________ (wait) for me when I ________________ (arrive) at the station.

b) "What ________________ (you, do) at this time last Monday?"

"I ________________ (be) asleep."

c) "________________ (you, go out) last night?"

"No, I ________________ (be) too tired."

d) "How fast ________________ (you, drive) when the accident

________________ (happen)?"

e) John ________________ (take) a photograph of her while she

________________ (not look).

f) I ________________ (walk) along the street when I suddenly

________________ (hear) footsteps behind me. somebody

________________ (follow) me.

g) Yesterday evening I ________________ (drop) a plate when I

________________ (do) the washing up. Fortunately it

________________ (not break).

können

/16

5 **Listen to the track *King Henry* on the CD.**
Then answer the questions in complete sentences. Use your exercise-book.

01

a) Why does King Henry stand out as a giant among English kings?
b) What is said about young Henry?
c) Which two reasons for his political decisions are mentioned in the text?
d) What happened in England because of the conflict with Rome?

/8

erreichte Punktzahl

/ 68

2 Present perfect, past perfect, future

Present perfect

Bildung des *present perfect*

have/has (bei *he, she, it*) + *past participle* → (1) regelmäßige Verben: ***infinitive*** + ***-ed*** / → (2) unregelmäßige Verben: ***3rd form***

(1) *We **have** wash**ed** our car.*

(2) *John **has** **bought** some books.*

Das *present perfect* bilden wir mit *have* oder *has* (bei *he, she, it*) und dem *past participle*. Bei der Bildung des *past participle* unterscheiden wir zwischen **regelmäßigen** und **unregelmäßigen** Verben.

- Regelmäßige Verben bilden wir mit der Grundform des Verbs und der Endung *-ed*.
- Unregelmäßige Verben haben Sonderformen, die man auswendig lernen muss. In deinem Schulbuch findest du eine Liste der unregelmäßigen Verben bestehend aus drei Formen (z. B. *to go, went, gone*). Die 3. Form ist immer die Past-Participle-Form (z. B. *gone*).

Verneinung und Frage

Da die Zeitform mit einem Hilfsverb *(to have)* gebildet wird kann dieses für die Verneinung (haven't/hasn't) (1) und auch für die Fragestellung (2) benutzt werden.

(1) *They **haven't** (= have not) arriv**ed** yet.*
*She **hasn't** (= has not) **done** her homework.*

(2) ***Have** you **seen** the new Bond-film?*
***Has** he clean**ed** the windows?*

Verwendung des *present perfect*

Das *present perfect* wird verwendet, wenn eine Handlung oder ein Zustand

(1) gerade eben erst beendet wurde (häufig mit *just*),
(2) zwar beendet wurde, aber Auswirkungen auf die Gegenwart hat,
(3) schon einmal oder bis jetzt noch nie passiert ist (ohne genaue Zeitangaben),
(4) in der Vergangenheit begonnen hat und immer noch (also in der Gegenwart) andauert.

(1) *They have just left.*
(2) *I have washed my car. It's clean now.*
(3) *John has never been to England./Have you ever seen a Bond movie?/ I have done it before, so it shouldn't be a problem.*
(4) *They have lived in Germany since 1977.*

Present perfect progressive

Bildung des *present perfect progressive*

have/has been *+ Infinitive +* ***ing***

(1) *Tom **has been** listen**ing** to the CD for hours.*

(2) *We'**ve been** sleep**ing** all morning. Now we're ready to go.*

Das ***present perfect progressive*** besteht aus einer Form von *to be* im ***present perfect*** (has/have been) und der Grundform des Verbs, an welches die Endung *-ing* angehängt wird.

Verneinung und Frage

Da die Zeitform mit einem Hilfsverb *(to be)* gebildet wird, kann dieses für die Verneinung *(hasn't/haven't been)* (1) und auch für die Fragestellung (2) benutzt werden.

(1) *They **haven't been** (= have not been) watch**ing** TV.*
*She **hasn't been** (= has not been) work**ing** this morning.*

(2) ***Have** you **been** listen**ing** to me?*
***Has** he **been** play**ing** football since two o'clock?*

Ausnahmen

Verben, die **Zustände** (1) oder **Sinneswahrnehmungen** (2) ausdrücken, stehen nie im **progressive**.

(1) z. B.: *to belong* (gehören), *to contain* (beinhalten), *to know* (wissen), *to love* (lieben), *to like* (mögen), *to need* (brauchen)

(2) z. B.: *to see* (sehen), *to smell* (riechen), *to hear* (hören)

Verwendung des *present perfect progressive*

Das *present perfect progressive* wird verwendet, wenn etwas

(1) in der Vergangenheit begonnen hat und immer noch andauert oder

(2) gerade eben erst beendet wurde (häufig mit *just*).

In beiden Fällen wird der Verlauf der Handlung betont.

(1) She has been playing tennis for three hours.

(2) We have just been painting the walls.

Present perfect mit *since* und *for*

Sowohl *present perfect (simple)* als auch das *present perfect progressive* stehen häufig zusammen mit den Präpositionen *since* und *for*.
Beide Präpositionen werden mit **„seit"** ins Deutsche übersetzt.

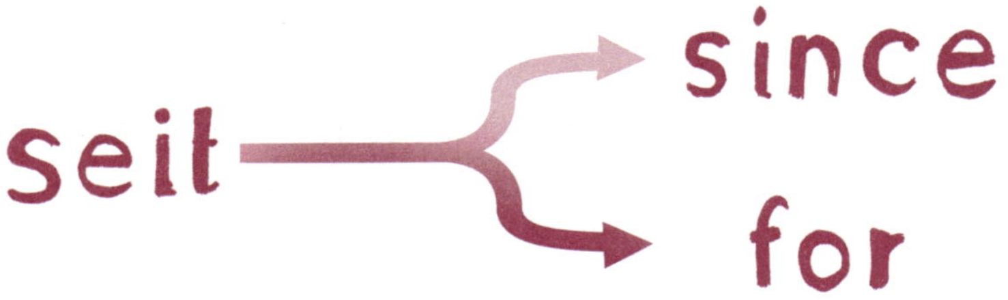

Since wird benutzt, wenn ein **Zeitpunkt, ab** dem etwas geschehen ist, genannt wird:

- Es wird eine Handlung beschrieben, die zu einem bestimmten Zeitpunkt in der Vergangenheit begann *(six o'clock/yesterday/last Christmas)* und bis zur Gegenwart andauert.
  I've been here since six o'clock. He has been waiting for you since yesterday.
- Soll dabei betont werden, dass die Handlung seit diesem Zeitpunkt ununterbrochen im Gange war, so wird *present perfect progressive* verwendet:
  He has been working on his car since lunch.
- Findet eine Handlung seit einem genannten Zeitpunkt in der Vergangenheit dagegen nicht ununterbrochen, aber z. B. immer wieder oder regelmäßig statt, so verwendet man eher das *present perfect (simple)*.
  She has run marathons since last Christmas.

For wird verwendet, wenn ein **Zeitraum, in** dem etwas geschehen ist, genannt wird:

- Es wird eine Handlung beschrieben, die zum Zeitpunkt des Sprechens schon eine bestimmte Zeit lang andauert *(ten minutes/ten days/hours)*, wobei aber der genaue Zeitpunkt ihres Beginns in der Vergangenheit nicht oder nur indirekt genannt wird.
  I've been jumping up and down for five minutes.
- Soll betont werden, dass diese Handlung tatsächlich während des genannten Zeitraums bis in die Gegenwart angedauert hat (und noch andauert), wird *present perfect progressive* verwendet.
  We have been playing cards for more than two hours.
- Findet eine Handlung über den genannten Zeitraum in der Vergangenheit bis in die Gegenwart regelmäßig immer wieder statt, verwendet man *present perfect (simple)*.
  We've travelled to Ibiza every July for ten years.

Past perfect/past perfect progressive

Bildung des *past perfect*

had + past participle

(1) *They **had** clean**ed** the windows.*

(2) *Sarah **had written** an e-mail.*

Das ***past perfect*** bilden wir mit *had* und dem ***past participle***. Bei der Bildung des *past participle* unterscheiden wir zwischen **regelmäßigen** und **unregelmäßigen** Verben.

- Regelmäßige Verben bilden wir mit der Grundform des Verbs und der Endung *-ed*.
- Unregelmäßige Verben haben Sonderformen, die man auswendig lernen muss. In deinem Schulbuch findest du eine Liste der unregelmäßigen Verben bestehend aus drei Formen (z. B. *to see, saw, seen*). Die 3. Form ist immer die *past-participle-form* (z. B. *seen*).

Verneinung und Frage

Da die Zeitform mit einem Hilfsverb *(to have)* gebildet wird, kann dieses für die Verneinung *(hadn't)* (1) und auch für die Fragestellung (2) benutzt werden.

(1) *We **hadn't** (= had not) arriv**ed**.*

(2) ***Had** you **bought** a hammer?*
*Why **hadn't** you clos**ed** the windows?*

Verwendung des *past perfect*

Das ***past perfect*** wird verwendet, wenn eine Handlung oder ein Zustand

(1) **vor** einer anderen in der Vergangenheit abgeschlossenen Handlung stattfanden,

(2) **vor** einem bestimmten Zeitpunkt in der Vergangenheit angefangen haben und zu diesem Zeitpunkt immer noch andauern.

(1) *Before he went home John **had called** his parents.*

(2) *They **had lived** in New York for years when they first visited Liberty Island.*

Die Handlung, die weniger weit zurück liegt, steht im ***simple past***.

Past perfect progressive

Bildung des *past perfect progressive*
had been + *Infinitive* + ***ing***
*John **had been** drink**ing** tea when his mother came home.*

Das *past perfect progressive* besteht aus einer Form von *to be* im *past perfect (had been)* und der Grundform des Verbs, an welche die Endung *-ing* angehängt wird.

Verneinung und Frage
Da die Zeitform mit einem Hilfsverb *(to be)* gebildet wird, kann dieses für die Verneinung *(hadn't been)* und auch für die Fragestellung benutzt werden.

Ausnahmen
Verben die **Zustände** oder **Sinneswahrnehmungen** ausdrücken stehen **nie** im ***progressive***!

Verwendung des *past perfect progressive*
Das *past perfect progressive* wird verwendet, wenn eine Handlung oder ein Vorgang **vor einem bestimmten Zeitpunkt der Vergangenheit** begonnen hatte und **bis zu diesem Zeitpunkt andauerte. Besonders betont** wird dabei der **Verlauf der Handlung**.
*They **had been** watch**ing** TV for hours when the telephone rang.*
*I **had been** work**ing** on the project since early December when I finally got some positive feedback.*

Test 1: *Present perfect/simple past*

1 **Put the verb in brackets into the correct tense *(present perfect* or *simple past).* Watch out for signal words.**

We ________________ (live) in England for almost a year and during that time we ________________ (learn) a lot about England and its people. We ________________ (be) to nice pubs and we ________________ (eat) fish and chips, which is really delicious. Last Christmas we even ________________ (try) Christmas pudding. We ________________ (visit) a number of famous sights and ________________ (travel) to beautiful towns, but we ________________ (not, meet) the Queen yet. We ________________ (enjoy) our time here but we ________________ (not, find) a good job anywhere. So last week we ________________ (decide) that we will move back to Germany.

2 **Complete the following questions and answers. Use the *present perfect* or the *simple past*.**

Tom: "________________________________ (you, ever, be) to England?"

Sarah: "Yes, ________________________________ (live) there for almost a year."

Tom: "And ________________________________ (you, meet) the Queen?"

Sarah: "No, unfortunately I ________________________ (not meet) the Queen."

Tom: "When ________________________________ (you, return) to Germany?"

Sarah: "We ____________________________ (return) to Germany a week ago."

Tom: "Why ____ (you, come back)?"

Sarah: "Well, it's because ____________________________ (cannot find) a good job anywhere."

Test 2: *Present perfect progressive*

1 **Complete the following sentences.**
Use the *present perfect progressive* and the verbs given.

watch ▪ work (2x) ▪ talk ▪ jump ▪ revise ▪ play ▪ do (2x) ▪ read

a) What ______________________________ (you) all day?

b) I ______________________________ in the garden all morning.

c) My mother ______________________________ this new book for weeks.

d) John ______________________________ computer games all the time.

e) My father ______________________________ on a model spaceship for days.

f) Anna ______________________________ vocabulary since breakfast.

g) Our dog ______________________________ around in the garden for two hours.

h) Aunt Audrey ______________________________ TV for hours.

i) We ______________________________ (just) about what

you ______________________________ all day.

2 **Put the verbs in brackets into the correct tense. Decide whether you need *present perfect* or *present perfect progressive*.**

John ________________ (do) his homework quickly. He is finished now. But Jack ________________ (waste) a lot of time, because he ____________________ (watch) TV all afternoon. John ____________________ (just, phone) his friend Peter and they ____________________ (discuss) plans for the evening since then. Meanwhile Jack ____________________ (work) rapidly on his homework to catch up with his brother.

3 **Translate into English.**
Decide whether you need *present perfect* or *present perfect progressive*.

a) Ich wohne schon seit 1995 in dieser Stadt.

b) Mit diesem Buch habe ich noch nie gearbeitet.

c) Bist du schon einmal in den USA gewesen?

d) Tom ist gerade am Bahnhof angekommen.

e) Er ist noch nie einen Marathon gelaufen.

f) Ich kann diese CD nicht kaufen, weil ich schon mein ganzes Geld ausgegeben habe.

g) Wir haben noch nicht entschieden, was wir machen wollen.

h) Hast du deine Hausaufgaben noch nicht gemacht?

i) Sie spielen bereits seit drei Stunden Fußball.

4 **Write an e-mail (about 80 words) to your friend in London. Tell him/her what has happened at school and at home since his/her last mail. Also ask him/her about his/her experiences.**
Use the *simple past,* the *present perfect* and the *present perfect progressive* as often as possible.

Hi ______________________ ,

___

___

___

___

___

___

___

___

___

___

___

___

___

üben

questions and sentences in the *past perfect (simple)*.

ıomans played an important role in British history.

____

____

How did they reach the British Isles?

____

____

c) The Romans came to Britain by ship.

____

____

d) What did the Romans do in Britain?

____

____

e) They beat the Celts in most battles, but they didn't conquer the whole country.

____

____

f) Did the Romans learn the Celtic language?

____

____

g) No, they didn't learn the Celtic language but spoke Latin.

____

____

h) Did the Romans found important cities in Britain?

____

____

i) The teacher didn't say anything about cities, but he said they built a lot of important roads.

____

____

üben

2 **Complete the following text.**
Use the *simple past, past perfect* or *past perfect progressive forms* of the verbs in brackets.

The Celts ______________ (come) to Britain 2500 years ago. Some of them ______________ (live) in Western Europe, others ________________ (stay) in Central Europe before they ________________ (begin) to settle in Britain. The Celts ______________________ (live) in Britain for about six centuries before the Romans _________________ (arrive). Because the Romans ________________ ________________ (beat) the Celts in lots of battles, the Celts ________________ (have to) get along with the Romans. The Celts already ______________________ (settle) there for more than 1000 years before the Angles and Saxons ________________ (come) to Britain. Before they ________________ (go) to the British Isles, they ______________ (live) in what is today Denmark and Northern Germany. Because the Celts ________________ (lose) battles against the Angles and Saxons, they ________________ (move) west to the hills of Cornwall, Scotland and Wales.

3 **Translate into English. Decide whether you need *simple past* or *past perfect*.**

a) Obwohl die Kelten schreckliche Krieger gewesen waren, fürchteten die Römer sie nicht.

b) Nachdem die Römer große Teile Englands erobert hatten, heirateten viele von ihnen keltische Frauen.

c) In Schottland gab es kaum römische Einflüsse, da sie den Hadrians-Wall nicht überwunden hatten *(to get across)*.

d) Obwohl die Römer erfolgreich gewesen waren, lernten die Kelten ihre Sprache nicht.

Klassenarbeit Nr. 2

45 min

1 **Use the verb in the correct tense (***present perfect simple, present perfect progressive, simple past)* **and put in** ***since*** **and** ***for*** **where necessary.**

At the weight-loss camp

Darren ____________________ (always, want) to spend a holiday at an adventure camp, and now he ____________________ (be) at Brecon Beacon weight loss camp ____________________ almost a week.

He ____________________ (do) lots of activities and he ____________________ (meet) some nice people. He even says he ____________________ (enjoy) most of the time at the camp. Yesterday, all the kids ____________________ (sit) around a camp fire. Darren ____________________ (talk) to Liz all evening.

He ____________________ (know) her since last Saturday, but everybody could see that he liked her very much. On Monday, Darren ____________________ (learn) a lot about cooking healthy meals and he ____________________ (find out) that he could even like it. This ____________________ (be) a new experience for a boy who ____________________ (eat) only junk food or ____________________ (put) TV dinners into the microwave all his life. There ____________________ (be) a lot more things for him to learn ____________________ he ____________________ (come) to the camp.

For example, walking up and down the hills ____________________ more than three hours ____________________ (be) an experience his feet won't forget so quickly … Darren ____________________ (plan) to do more sport, but it will take a long time before he can wear T-shirts a normal size.

/20

können

2 **Fill in the correct form of the verb and *since* or *for*.**
More about weight-loss camps

a) ____________________ 1999 seven weight-loss camps ____________________ (open) in the UK.

b) Darren ____________________ (do) any sport ____________________ he has weighed more than 100 kg.

c) The teenagers at the camp ____________________ (play) rugby ____________________ one hour everyday ____________________ the day they arrived.

d) Darren ____________________ (lose) 7 kg ____________________ the day he came to the camp.

e) He ____________________ (not, eat) any chips ____________________ six weeks.

/ 11

erreichte Punktzahl
/ 31

verstehen

3 Future

Will-future

Bildung des *will-future*

will + ***Infinitive*** (Grundform des Verbs)

*I **will go** shopping.*

*They **will be** back in a minute.*

Verneinung und Frage

Da die Zeitform mit dem modalen Hilfsverb *will* gebildet wird, muss dieses auch für die Verneinung *(won't = will not)* (1) und die Fragestellung (2) benutzt werden.

(1) *They won't (will not) be home before midnight.*

(2) *Will you watch the show?*

Verwendung des *will-future*

Das *will-future* wird verwendet für

(1) Vermutungen, Vorhersagen oder Prognosen über ein zukünftiges Geschehen,

(2) für zukünftige Ereignisse, auf die der Sprecher keinen Einfluss hat.

(1) *The weather will be fine tomorrow. I think he will finish the job.*

(2) *John will take his exam in June. My sister will be eighteen next year.*

Going-to-future

Bildung des *going-to-future*

Form von to be + ***going to*** + ***Infinitive*** (Grundform des Verbs)

*It's **going to rain**.*

*We are **going to fly** to London next weekend.*

Verneinung und Frage

Da die Zeitform mit einem Hilfsverb *(to be)* gebildet wird, kann dieses für die Verneinung *(am not, isn't, aren't)* (1) und auch für die Fragestellung (2) benutzt werden.

(1) *It isn't **going to rain**.*

(2) *What is he **going to do**?*

Verwendung

Das *going-to-future* wird verwendet, um

(1) auszudrücken, was jemand (in der Zukunft) zu tun beabsichtigt (a) oder fest plant (b), um

(2) auszudrücken, dass etwas bald geschehen wird, weil es dafür bereits Anzeichen gibt.

(1) a) *John **is going to repair** his bike.*
John hat vor, sein Fahrrad zu reparieren.

b) *They **are going to fly** to New York next month.*
The have already ordered the tickets.

(2) *Look at the sky! It's **going to snow**.*

Future with the simple present

Häufig verwendete Verben in dieser Funktion sind *arrive, begin, end, land, leave, start.*

Zukünftiges Geschehen kann auch mit dem *simple present* ausgedrückt werden, wenn der **Sprecher dieses nicht beeinflussen kann**, wie dies z. B. bei Fahrplänen oder anderen festgelegten Zeitplänen der Fall sein kann *(time table future)*.

My train arrives in thirty minutes.

The film starts in half an hour.

Future with the present progressive

Zukünftige Handlungen können auch mit dem *present progressive* ausgedrückt werden, wenn diese (meist unter Mitwirkung des Sprechers) festgelegt oder vereinbart wurden *(diary future)*.

We are celebrating our wedding in May next year.

I am meeting my old teacher next Saturday.

üben

Test 1: *Will-future*

1 **Fill in the forms of the *will-future* for the horoscope.**

Taurus (between April 21 and May 21): You won't like (not like) your family's plans for the weekend, but nobody will ask (ask) your opinion. You ______________ (meet) someone nice at a party, but he/she ______________ (be) very shy. Sunday ______________ (not be) very exciting, a good opportunity to relax!

Gemini (between May 21 and June 21): You ______________ (hear) some news you ______________ (not believe) at first, but you ______________ (realize) it is the bitter truth. An old friend you have always trusted ______________ (have) the unpleasant duty of revealing the secret to you. Your life ______________ (change) dramatically on Sunday!

2 **Complete the following dialogue. Use *will* or *won't* with the verbs in brackets.**

John: "Martin is in our football team. Will you come (you, come) with me to his match tomorrow afternoon?"

Dave: "No, I won't come (not come). I'm more into tennis."

John: "Oh, come on. It's Martin's first big match. We must cheer him. And I'm sure it will be (be) a lot of fun."

Dave: "By the way, when will it start (it, start)?"

John: "I think it will begin (begin) at 3 o'clock."

Dave: "Well, there's a problem. Every Thursday I have piano lessons at four. My parents won't be (not be) happy if I miss one of them."

John: "Ok, you could only watch the first half."

Dave: "Ok then. But you will have (have) to pick me up. I don't know the way to the stadium."

John: "No problem. I will pick (pick) you up half an hour before the match. See you tomorrow. I'm sure you won't regret (not regret) it."

Test 2: *Going-to-future*

üben

1 **Say or ask what the people are going to do.**

a) Jack is going to buy (buy) some ice-cream?

b) Linda isn't going to watch (not watch) the basketball match.

c) What are you to do (you, do) next weekend?

d) Jake and Tom are going to join (join) the chess club.

e) My father is going to sell (sell) his car.

f) When are they going to fly (they, fly) to Italy?

g) I am going to repair (repair) my motorbike.

h) This year we aren't going to visit (not visit) our relatives in England.

2 **Translate into English.**

a) Mein Vater wird heute nachmittag das Auto waschen.

my father is going to wash his car

b) Meine Mutter wird morgen die Garage aufräumen. Ich habe nicht vor, ihr zu helfen.

c) Wann wird dein Bruder den Garten aufräumen?

d) Werden wir eine Gartenparty machen? Ja.

e) Dann werde ich einige Kekse backen.

Test 3: *Going-to-future and will future*

1 **Complete the following dialogue. Use *going-to-future* or *will-future*.**

Plans for the weekend

It's Friday afternoon. Sally, Max and Robin are talking about their plans for the weekend:

Sally: "What ______________________ (you, do) tomorrow, Robin?"

Robin: "I'm not sure, but I heard the weather forecast this morning. Tomorrow it ______________________ (not, rain).
It ______________________ (be) a sunny day. So I think
I ______________________ (go swimming)."

Max: "Great idea, but I'm afraid I can't come. I've already packed my suitcase, because this weekend ______________________ (we, visit) my aunt in Scotland."

2 **Complete the questions. Use *going-to-future* or *will-future*.**

a) What ______________________________________ tomorrow?
I am going **to see the doctor.**

b) ____?
I'm going to do my homework **after dinner**.

c) ______________________ help you? I suppose **John** will help me.

d) ____?
I'm going to work with him **in my room**.

3 **Listen to the track *The Channel Tunnel* on the CD.**
Then write from dictation.

02

Klassenarbeit Nr. 3 30 min

können

1 **Susanne and her younger sister Sabine want to visit their English cousin Sally in Dover. Since Sabine has not started learning English yet, Susanne has to sum up the main information from her telephone conversation with Sally to her sister in German. You are Susanne. Don't translate every word, but get the message across.**

Susanne: We want to visit you in England. Are you home?
Sally: Yes, we are all home next week. You're welcome!

Susanne: Sie sagt, ______________________________

____

Sabine: Super. Frag doch mal, wie das Wetter werden soll.

Susanne: Great! ______________________________

______________________________?

Sally: I've heard it will be cloudy and windy. Usually the weather isn't so nice here in May.

Susanne: Sie sagt, ______________________________

____

Sabine: Kannst du sie fragen, ob man schon im Meer schwimmen kann?

Susanne: Sabine wants to know ______________________________

______________________________?

Sally: No, I suppose it will be too cold. Will Sabine come, too?

Susanne: Yes, ______________________________.

Sabine, sie sagt, dass ______________________________

Sabine: Oh, sehr schade. Wird sie uns vom Bahnhof abholen?

Susanne: Sally, ______________________________?

Sally: Well, when does your train arrive at Dover?

Susanne: Sie will wissen, ______________________________.

Sabine: Das werden wir erst wissen, wenn wir am Bahnhof gefragt haben.

Susanne: Sabine says, ______________________________.

Sally: Don't arrive before twelve o'clock because nobody will be home until then.

Susanne: Sie sagt ______________________________.

Sabine: Alles klar.

/10

2 Find suitable questions.

a) ______________________________ at the weekend?

I'm going to visit my aunt.

b) ______________________________? The weather won't be too nice on Monday.

c) ______________________________?

We will need about £20.

/3

3 Complete the following sentences by using the words in brackets in their correct form.

Be careful of the different possibilities of expressing the future.
Use either *will-future, going-to-future, present progressive* or *simple present*.

a) Tom: "I think, I ______________ (call) Jane tomorrow."

b) Jane: "We ______________ (climb) in the mountains next weekend."

c) Her birthday ______________ (be) next Wednesday.

d) Jill: "We ______________ (fly) to Chicago this summer. I've already bought the tickets."

e) On Monday I ______________ (see) the doctor.

f) It's rather cold. It ______________ (snow) soon.

g) Bond: "I have to hurry. The train ______________ (leave) at half past two this afternoon."

h) John: "Don't worry. I ______________ (do) the shopping for you."

i) The German team ______________ (not, win) a gold medal.

/9

erreichte Punktzahl
/ 22

verstehen

4 *Auxiliaries*

Hilfsverben: *auxiliaries*

Es wird grundsätzlich zwischen den **Hilfsverben** *do, have, be* und den **modalen Hilfsverben** *must, can, need to, may, shall* ... unterschieden.

Hilfsverben *do/have und be*

Do (tun), *have* (haben) und *be* (sein) sind sowohl Hilfs- als auch Vollverben. Als Vollverben können sie alleine stehen, alle Zeiten bilden und werden wörtlich ins Deutsche übersetzt. Als Hilfsverben verlieren sie ihre Eigenbedeutung und werden als Teil des Prädikats zur Zeitenbildung benötigt, wobei sie immer mit einem Vollverb zusammenstehen müssen. Einzige Ausnahme sind hier die Kurzantworten.

Modale Hilfsverben

Ein **modales Hilfsverb** fügt der Satzaussage immer eine weitere Bedeutung hinzu bzw. ändert diese. Durch Verwendung eines modalen Hilfsverbs lassen sich verschiedene Sprechabsichten (Erlaubnis, Verbot, Vermutung, Ratschlag, Bitte, Vorschlag ...), aber auch Fähigkeiten, Notwendigkeiten und Zwänge formulieren. Alle *modal auxiliaries* haben folgende Eigenschaften:

- Sie sind **unveränderlich**, das heißt, in der 3. Person Singular wird **kein *-s*** angehängt und es gibt **keine *ing*-Form.**
- Nur bei Fragen und Kurzantworten können *modal auxiliaries* alleine stehen, sonst müssen sie – anders als ihre deutschen Entsprechungen – **immer mit dem Infinitiv eines Vollverbs zusammen stehen.**
- Sie dürfen bei Fragen und Verneinungen **nicht mit *to do* umschrieben** werden.
- Sie können **nicht als Infinitiv** und **nicht für alle Zeiten** verwendet werden. Hier werden entsprechende Ersatzformen benutzt.

Müssen: *must/have to/need not to*

Mit *must* (müssen) und der Ersatzform *have to* (*must* kann nur im Präsens verwendet werden) werden folgende Sprechabsichten formuliert:

- **Zwang** oder **Notwendigkeit**
  He has to go now or he will miss the last bus home.
  I must sleep more to stay healthy.
- **große Wahrscheinlichkeit**
  Your grades are excellent. You must be very proud.
- **nachdrücklicher Ratschlag**
  This book is brilliant. You must read it. Your car is a wreck. You have to sell it.

Die **Verneinung** erfolgt über *need not* oder *do not have to:*
You need not speak so loud. I'm not deaf.
You do not have to speak so loud. – Du brauchst nicht so laut sprechen. Ich bin nicht taub.

Achtung: Die Verneinung ist nicht mustn't (was ein Verbot ausdrücken würde): You mustn't speak loud in the library. – Du darfst in der Bücherei nicht laut sprechen.

Können: *can/could/be able to*

Can/could/be able to/be allowed to werden im Deutschen mit **können** wiedergegeben, im Englischen muss je nach Bedeutung unterschieden werden.

- **Können** im Sinne von **imstande sein**, etwas zu tun: *can* oder *be able to.*
  I can swim. But I am not able to swim across the Channel.
  Die Ersatzform *able to* wird im *present* nur benutzt, wenn betont werden soll, dass jemand zu etwas wirklich (nicht) imstande ist, sonst wird sie für die übrigen Zeiten verwendet.
- **Können** im Sinne einer bestehenden Möglichkeit: *can* und *could.*
  We can take the ferry. But if you get seasick, we could also take the train instead.
  Could hat hier die Bedeutung des Konjunktivs (= Möglichkeitsform), nicht der Vergangenheit! Ob Konjunktiv oder *past tense* gemeint ist, muss aus dem Zusammenhang erschlossen werden.
- **Können** im Sinne einer **Bitte** oder eines **Wunsches**: *can* und *could.*
  Dad, can I go to England in summer? Could you give me more pocket-money?
  Diese Formen verwendet man nur in der Grundform. Hier sind keine Ersatzformen möglich.

Dürfen: *can/may/be allowed to/must not*

Can/be allowed to drücken eine Erlaubnis aus:
You can take photos inside /You are allowed to take photos inside.

Cannot/can't bzw. ***not be allowed to*** wird verwendet, wenn die Erlaubnis nicht gewährt wird:
We are not allowed to cycle here/We cannot (can't) cycle here.

Can, may und *must not* können nur im *simple present* verwendet werden. Für die Vergangenheit und Zukunft wird die Ersatzform *be allowed to* verwendet.

- bei einem echten (bzw. förmlicheren) Verbot verwendet man ***must not***:
  You mustn't drive without a driver's licence.
- ***May*** steht für eine förmlicher ausgedrückte Erlaubnis (1) (*be allowed to* ist weniger formell) und wird verwendet, wenn man um Erlaubnis bittet (2) (*can* ist weniger formell):
  (1) *You may sit here.*
  (2) *May I use your pen?*

Im Präsidentschaftswahlkampf 2008 verwendete der spätere US-Präsident Barack Obama den Slogan *Yes, we can.*

Can verlangt als modales Hilfsverb eigentlich ein Vollverb. Dem scheint Obamas Slogan zu widersprechen. In der (politischen) Werbung wird teilweise (spielerisch) mit der Sprache umgegangen.

Daher heißt es für Schulaufgaben auf jeden Fall: *Yes, we can. But not in the test.*

Should/ought to

Die *modal auxiliaries should* und *ought to* werden verwendet, um
- eine **Verpflichtung**,
- eine **Wahrscheinlichkeit** oder
- einen **Rat** auszudrücken.

Im Deutschen verwenden wir dafür *sollten* oder *müssten.*
We should/ought to care more about the environment.
John should/ought to be home by five o'clock.
You should/ought to get some fresh air in here.

Als Ersatzform für beide *auxiliaries* wird *(not) to be supposed to* verwendet.

May/might/must not

Die *modal auxiliaries may/might/must not* werden verwendet, um **Erlaubnis oder Verbot** auszudrücken, und können in der Grundform nur im *simple present* verwendet werden.

- ***May:*** Wird verwendet, um **eine formale Erlaubnis** auszudrücken.
  You may borrow my car. – Du darfst mein Auto ausleihen.
  Die weniger förmliche Ersatzform für *may* in dieser Bedeutung ist ***to be allowed***.
  You are allowed to borrow my car.
- ***Might:*** Wird verwendet, um eine **Möglichkeit oder Vermutung** auszudrücken.
  She might give me her car today. – Vielleicht gibt sie mir heute ihr Auto.
  Hier gibt es **keine Ersatzform**, *might* kann also nur im *simple present* verwendet werden.
- ***Must not:*** Wird verwendet, um **ein formales Verbot** auszudrücken.
  You mustn't give her your car. She hasn't got a driving licence.
  Die weniger förmliche Ersatzform für *must not* in dieser Bedeutung ist *not to be allowed:*
  You are not allowed to borrow my car.

Test 1: *Auxiliaries do, have, be*

üben

1 **Underline the forms of the verbs *do, have* and *be* when used as *auxiliary verbs* in black, and in red when they are *used as full verbs*.**

Libby and Anna are doing a project on Martin Waldseemüller for school. They have already found out a lot about his life and work. They are planning to make a big poster which has all the important facts and figures. At the moment they are writing down some dates. After they have written down the text, they are going to glue some pictures of Waldseemüller and his famous map of America on the poster, too. Before they did the written work, Libby and Anna had read a lot of books on the discovery of the New World because they had not heard the name Waldseemüller before. But Anna's grandfather, who has always been very interested in history, gave them some good advice on which books to read.

2 **Translation.**

a) Ich mache sonntags keine Hausaufgaben.

____

b) Ich werde meine Hausaufgaben morgen machen

____

____.

c) Bis Freitag werde ich meine Hausaufgaben gemacht haben.

____

____

d) Ich mache seit zwei Stunden Hausaufgaben und bin noch nicht fertig.

____

____

e) Ich hatte meine Hausaufgaben nicht gemacht, als der Lehrer danach fragte.

____

____

3 **Mediation. School rules. Explain the rules to your American exchange partner. You don't need to translate every single word, but your partner should understand what the rules are about. *Use auxiliaries* wherever necessary. Sometimes there is more than one possible solution. Write in your exercise book.**

a) Jeder Schüler muss eine saubere Schuluniform tragen.

____

b) Schüler dürfen im Unterricht keine Jeans und keine Turnschuhe tragen.

____

____

c) Jeder Schüler muss pünktlich sein.

____

d) Jeder sollte mit Respekt behandelt werden.

____

e) Niemand sollte den Unterricht stören.

____

f) Ältere Schüler dürfen die Cafeteria benutzen

____.

g) Jeder sollte seinen Müll selbst aufräumen.

____

h) Jüngere Schüler dürfen in den Pausen Fußball spielen.

____

i) Nach dem Unterricht muss jeder Schüler seinen Stuhl auf seinen Tisch stellen.

____

____

j) Während der Unterrichtsstunden muss jeder im Schulhaus ruhig sein.

____

____

k) Schüler und Lehrer dürfen in der Schule nicht rauchen.

____

Test 2: *Modal auxiliaries*

üben

1 **Read the sentences and tick the correct solution. Sometimes both are correct.**

a) Today I ☐ **can't** ☐ **am not able to** go to the youth club dance because my Dad said no.

b) He said I won't ☐ **be able** ☐ **be allowed to** go out again unless I do better at school.

c) Tom ☐ **mustn't** ☐ **doesn't have to** work today.

d) He ☐ **is allowed to** ☐ **is able to** stay home.

e) You ☐ **may** ☐ **must** use my car today. I don't need it.

f) Yesterday Tom ☐ **couldn't** ☐ **wasn't able to** play football because he was injured.

2 **Put the sentences into the tenses given in brackets.**

a) I can run a marathon (present perfect).

____

b) You can't run a marathon. (simple past)

____

c) You must leave now. (will-future)

____

d) You should do your homework. (past perfect)

____

e) Why must you see the doctor? (simple past)

____

f) I can see you tomorrow. (will-future)

____

g) John may visit you. (present perfect)

____

h) You ought to take the bus. (simple past)

____

i) Jane mustn't leave the house. (past perfect)

____

j) What should they do for the project? (will-future)

____

Klassenarbeit Nr. 4

30 min

können

1 **Put the sentences into the tenses given in brackets.**

a) I am doing a project for school. (present perfect)

____

b) You are late. (will-future)

____

c) You don't do your homework in time. (simple past)

____

d) Mike is a teacher. (going-to-future)

____

e) I have a great holiday job. (past perfect)

____

/10

2 **Translation. Use your exercise-book.**

a) Ich muss seit September mit dem Fahrrad in die Schule fahren.

____

b) Die Busfahrkarte ist so teuer geworden, dass ich sie seitdem nicht bezahlen kann.

____

____

c) Mein Vater konnte mich nicht mit seinem Auto fahren, weil er es selbst brauchte.

____

____

d) Möglicherweise kauft meine Mutter bald ein zweites Auto

____________________.

e) Dann werde ich nicht mehr den Bus nehmen müssen

____________________.

f) Ich hoffe, ich werde ihr Auto oft nehmen dürfen.

____

/12

können

3 **Fill in the correct *modal auxiliaries*.**

a) "Hi Mum. Your new car looks great. It ______________ have been very expensive."

b) "No, it was a special offer. I ______________ buy an expensive car."

c) "______________ I use it, too?"

d) "You ______________ use it but you ______________ always ask me first."

e) "And I ______________ need it myself most of the time.

/6

4 **Complete the following conversation.**
Use a form of *can, have to, be able to,* or *be allowed to.*

James Bond has just returned from a mission and is talking to his boss M.

M: "How did you get back without your car? "

Bond: "I simply ______________________ walk. There was no other way."

M: " __________ you ______________ finish your mission?"

Bond: "Of course, Sir. I __________________________ steal the CD you wanted. Here it is. By the way, __________________ I see my new car?"

M: "No, I'm afraid not. Q __________________________ do some other work first. But yesterday he showed me some of the new weapons for your car."

Bond: "Really? I ___________________________ (not) see them. He told me to come back later. I hope I ________________________ handle *(umgehen mit)* the new car by next weekend."

M: "I hope so, too. That's another very important mission for you. We ________________ (not) risk a failure *(Misserfolg)*."

/9

erreichte Punktzahl
/ 37

5 Conditional sentences

First conditional

Bildung

– Das ***first conditional*** wird mit dem *simple present* und *will-future* gebildet. In dem Teil des Satzes, der *if* enthält, wird das ***simple present*** benutzt, im anderen Teil des *first conditional*-Satzes wird das ***will-future*** benutzt. Grammatisch wird ein *first conditional*-Satz so gebildet:

If + subject + simple present	***subject + will-future***
If *I have time, ...*	*..., I* ***will*** *come to your party.*
If *I see her, ...*	*..., I* ***will*** *ask Sarah her opinion.*

Die zwei Satzteile können in beliebiger Reihenfolge stehen und sind dann durch ein Komma getrennt, wenn der *if*-Satz am Anfang steht, da andernfalls nicht schnell ersichtlich wäre, wo der *if*-Satz endet. Steht der *if*-Satz am Ende, ist durch das Wörtchen *if* die Grenze des Teilsatzes sofort zu erkennen.
If *I have time, I* ***will*** *come to the party. I* ***will*** *stay at home* ***if*** *it rains.*
Nach dem Subjektpronomen wird *will* oft mit *'ll* abgekürzt und in negativen Sätze wird *will not* mit *won't* abgekürzt.
I will ⇒ I'll
You will ⇒ You'll
He will not ⇒ He won't
They will not ⇒ They won't

– **Verneinungen** können in einem oder in beiden Satzteilen stehen und folgen den normalen Regeln der Zeitform.
If it snows, I ***won't*** *play football. If it* ***doesn't*** *rain, I'll play tennis.*

– In **Entscheidungsfragen** bleibt der *if*-Satzteil gleich, aber *will* und Subjekt werden in ihrer Stellung vertauscht. Bei Ergänzungsfragen steht zusätzlich das **Fragewort** an erster Stelle im *will*-Satzteil:
Will ***you*** *say hello, if you see her?*
If they go to Italy, which sights ***will*** *they visit?*

Gebrauch

Das ***first conditional*** wird gebraucht, wenn

1. die beschriebene Situation **in der Zukunft** liegt.
   If it rains tomorrow, I'll need my umbrella.
2. die beschriebene Situation wirklich **möglich** ist (noch eintreten kann).
   I'll send you an email if I need help with English.
3. die beschriebene Situation **sehr wahrscheinlich** ist, nicht nur Fantasie.
   If he passes the English test, he'll celebrate with his friends.

Eine wichtige Funktion des *first conditional* ist, jemanden vor den Folgen seines Handelns zu **warnen**.
If you eat burgers and chips every day, you will become fat and unhealthy.

Second conditional

Bildung

- Das ***second conditional*** wird mit dem *simple past* und einem *would*-Satzteil gebildet. In dem Teil des Satzes, der *if* enthält, wird das ***simple past*** benutzt, und im anderen Teil des *second conditional*-Satzes wird *would* benutzt.
  Sätze im *second conditional* werden grammatisch so gebildet:

If + subject + simple past	***subject + would + infinitive***
If *I found £1000, …*	*…, I* ***would*** *buy lots of designer clothes.*
If *we threw a party at home, …*	*…, we* ***would*** *have to clean up the next morning.*

  Die zwei Satzteile können in beliebiger Reihenfolge stehen.
  If *I won the lotto, I* ***would*** *buy a computer.*
  I ***would*** *go to the cinema* ***if*** *they showed good films.*
  Nach dem Subjektpronomen wird *would* oft mit *'d* abgekürzt, und in negativen Sätze wird *would not* mit *wouldn't* abgekürzt:
  *I would ⇒ I'**d**, You would ⇒ You'**d**,*
  *He would not ⇒ He **wouldn't***

> Im Englischen existiert nur für das Verb **be** eine Konjunktivform. Deshalb steht oft im ***second conditional* were** statt des üblichen **was:** If I were, If she/he weren't, If it were …

- **Verneinungen können** in einem oder beiden Satzteilen stehen und folgen den normalen Regeln der Zeitform:
  *If it snowed, I **wouldn't** go to school.*
  *If they **weren't** so expensive, I'd buy a new mobile phone.*
- In **Entscheidungsfragen** bleibt der *if*-Satzteil gleich, aber *would* und Subjekt werden vertauscht. Bei Ergänzungsfragen steht zusätzlich das **Fragewort** an erster Stelle im *would*-Satzteil:
  Would he *help her if she asked him?*
  How *would he get here if he didn't have a car?*

Gebrauch

Das ***second conditional*** wird gebraucht, wenn

1. die beschriebene Situation **in der Zukunft** liegt.
   If it snowed tomorrow, school would be closed.
2. die beschriebene Situation noch **möglich**, allerdings **unwahrscheinlich** ist.
   If somebody shot me, it would hurt.
3. die beschriebene Situation ein **Wunsch** oder eine Fantasie/Vorstellung **in der Gegenwart** ist.
   If I had the chance, I'd marry Prince Harry.

Eine wichtige Funktion des *second conditional* ist, **Empfehlungen oder Ratschläge** auszudrücken, besonders, wenn man sich in die Lage eines anderen versetzt.
If I were you, I wouldn't eat so many burgers and chips.
I'd see the film in the original English version if I were you.

Test 1: *First conditional*

üben

1 **Match the halves of sentences to make suitable conditional clauses.**

If you join a club, ◇	◇ if he always eats lots of sweets.
I'll have the rest of the weekend free ◇	◇ if they go on holiday to London.
If we watch a horror film in the dark, ◇	◇ if I do all of my homework on Friday.
If she wins the modelling competition, ◇	◇ you'll meet lots of new friends.
They'll probably visit the London Eye ◇	◇ we'll get scared.
All his teeth will fall out ◇	◇ a magazine will definitely offer her a contract.

2 **Complete the sentences to warn your younger brother.**

a) If you play violent computer games, ______________________________

____

b) Your hair will fall out ______________________________

____

c) If you come home late, ______________________________

____

d) The teacher will be angry ______________________________

____

e) If you spend all of your money on clothes, ______________________________

____

f) If you don't install an internet firewall, ______________________________

____

3 **Welcome your exchange partner to your house. What will you say in English?**

a) Wenn du hungrig bist, wird meine Mutter etwas für dich kochen.

____

b) Wenn du Angst vor Hunden hast, werde ich unseren Rottweiler im Garten lassen.

____

c) Die Nachbarn werden sich beschweren, wenn wir die Musik zu laut spielen.

____

üben

Test 2: *Second conditional*

1 **Complete the following sentences by putting the words in brackets into the correct form. Use the *second conditional*.**

a) My dad gave me this ring. He ________________ (be) upset if I ________________ (lose) it.

b) If you ________________ (not pass) the exams, ________________ (repeat) the school year?

c) How ________________ (he/get home) if the busses ________________ (be) cancelled?

d) My bike is very old, I ________________ (not get) much money if I (sell) ________________ it.

e) ________________ (you lend) him money if he ________________ (ask) you?

2 **Complete the following dialogue. Use the words in brackets to build *conditional sentences* (type 2).**

Linda: "Shall we take the 7:00 bus?"

Jack: "No, if we took (take) it, we would arrive too early (arrive too early)."

Linda: "Why don't we follow my elder brother too the disco?"

Jack: "If we ________________ (follow) him, we ________________ (to get into trouble)."

Linda: "How shall we get home, by bus or by taxi?"

Jack: "If we ________________ (get home, taxi), ________________ (expensive)."

Linda: "Shall I ask Laura out from class 8A?"

Jack: "No, ________________ (say no), ________________ (be embarrassing)."

Linda: "Do you think I should wear a skirt or jeans to the party?"

Jack: "Jeans. ________________ (wear skirt), ________________ (get cold)."

3 **Your friend is complaining. Answer the following statements by using the second conditional.**

I am tired. I always stay up until midnight.

If you didn't stay up until midnight, you wouldn't be so tired.

a) I'm not in a club and never meet any new friends.

____

____

b) I love DVDs but I have hardly any money left at the end of the month.

____

____

c) I'm wearing my favourite skirt, but I really feel cold.

____

____

d) I have saved some money but I can't buy a new computer.

____

____

Klassenarbeit Nr. 5

60 min

können

1 **Complete the following sentences by putting the verbs in brackets into the correct form.**

a) I would fix your bike if I ____________________ (have) a screwdriver of the correct size, but I don't.

b) I ____________________ (make) a salad for the picnic if the tomatoes in my garden are ripe.

c) If you ____________________ (not do) more sport, you ____________________ (not feel) fitter.

d) If they ____________________ (live) closer, they ____________________ (see) each other more often.

e) What ____________________ (he/say) if he ________________ (know) you broke his computer?

f) If the house ____________________ (be) ever on fire, we ____________________ (escape) through the window.

/10

2 **Find and correct the mistakes in Sarah's email. There are six mistakes.**

To: myemail@emailme.com

From: Sarah123@emailfun.com

Hi! How are you? What have you been doing recently? I go to a party yesterday and met some boys. We were dancing, and one kissed my friend Lizzie. Then they had offered us vodka and the boy and Lizzie went outside. I wonder what they have done. There's another party this weekend, but shall I go? One guy is very attractive, but how can I tell if he likes me? If I drank vodka and wear a skirt, I would look cool. But I was not happy with drinking vodka. I don't think it's good to drink beer and then kiss boys, but if I warned Lizzie, she will think I'm annoying. What can I do? Write soon! Sarah

/12

können

3 **Read *All about Wales*. True or false? Correct the false sentences. Use your exercise book.**

All about Wales

Wales is one of the four nations that make up the United Kingdom. It is situated in the south-west of Great Britain. To the east of Wales, you find England, to the south you find the Bristol Channel, and to the north-east you find the River Dee. To the west and north of Wales is the Irish Sea and ferries run regularly across to Cork from Swansea, which is Wales' second-largest city. Since the 1800s, Wales has been an industrial state and still exports a lot of coal and steel. However, many factories and mines were closed down in the 1980s by the Conservative government, and the service industry became more important. Most of the Welsh population lives in the valleys and the coastal areas of South Wales. Other areas, in Mid Wales, the south west and west, are mainly hilly countryside areas. The capital city of Wales is Cardiff (in Welsh "Caerdydd"), which became the capital in 1955 and is also in the south. In this area, English is the most commonly used language, although a separate Welsh language exists and all official documents and road-signs are bilingual. A separate parliament for Wales, the "National Assembly", was formed in 1999, and has limited power to pass laws independent of the main U.K. Parliament in London. The Welsh people like to preserve their cultural identity. They learn and speak Welsh, have had their own history of literature since the 5th century, and hold huge celebrations for Saint David's Day (the Patron Saint of Wales) every year on the 1st of March. They wear traditional dress and eat traditional foods, such as Welsh cakes, rye bread, faggots, Welsh rarebit (cheese on toast) and corned-beef pasties. Wales is also famous for choirs, sheep, rugby, whisky and mountain trekking, a perfect destination for your family holiday!

		true	false
a)	If you travel east from Wales, you will be in Ireland.	☐	☐
b)	If you are in Wales on 1st March, you will see people eating rabbits.	☐	☐
c)	You would see signs in Welsh and English, if you travelled to Wales.	☐	☐
d)	If you see signs for *Cardiff*, you are in the north of Wales.	☐	☐
e)	If you go to the Welsh countryside, you will see lots of sheep.	☐	☐

/8

können

4 **Read *All about Wales*. What happened in these years? Write in full sentences.**

a) 600s ______________________________

____

b) 1800s ______________________________

____

c) 1980s ______________________________

____

d) 1955 ______________________________

____

e) 1999 ______________________________

____

/10

5 **Answer the following questions with at least *four conditional sentences* each. You can use the pictures to help you. Use your exercise book.**

a) What would you buy, if you had £10,000 to spend?

b) If you were 70 years old, what would you do in your free time? With whom?

/16

erreichte Punktzahl

/ 56

Klassenarbeit Nr. 6

45 min

können

1 **Welcome your exchange partner to your house. What will you say?**

	German	English
a)	*Wenn du irgendwas nicht verstehst, werde ich es für dich übersetzen.*	
b)	*Wenn du dein MP3-Player dabei hättest, könnten wir Musik austauschen.*	
c)	*Du wirst meinen Freund kennen lernen, wenn wir in die Disko gehen.*	
d)	*Wenn du keine Hausschuhe anziehst, werden deine Füße kalt werden.*	
e)	*Wenn meine Mutter nicht so streng wäre, müssten wir nicht so früh ins Bett gehen.*	

/10

2 **Make up *first conditional sentences* to tell your friend about sport and health. Use the pictures to help you.**

a) If you  ______________________, you  ______________________.

b) If you  ______________________, you 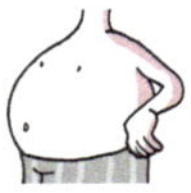 ______________________.

c) You will  ______________________, if you  ______________________.

d) If you  ______________________, you  ______________________.

/8

3 **Listen to the track *Girl Bands* and answer the following questions:**

03

a) Who was involved in the experiment?

____

b) What did researchers want to find out?

____

____

c) What do the results of the experiment show?

____

____

/3

können

4 **Listen to *Girl Bands* again. True, false or not in the text?**

		true	false	not in the text
a)	If young girls watch pop videos, they will have to read a list of words.	☐	☐	☐
b)	If girl bands are popular for being slim and sexy, young girls will want to be like them.	☐	☐	☐
c)	Young girls will feel fat and unhappy, if they listen to the words of pop songs.	☐	☐	☐
d)	The Spice Girls wouldn't be so popular, if Victoria Beckham weren't so thin.	☐	☐	☐
e)	If young girls listened to songs without watching the videos, they wouldn't feel so bad about their body shape.	☐	☐	☐

/5

5 **Answer the following questions with at least *four conditional sentences*. Use your exercise book.**

Where would you travel to, if you could pick any country?
How would you get there?

6 **Write an email to your best friend and explain why you don't like his/her new girlfriend/boyfriend. What might some consequences of their relationship be? Write at least *four conditional* sentences.**

File Edit Merge Insert Tools Plug-ins Setup Help

To: myemail@emailme.com

From: bestmate4eva@goldemail.com

____

____

____

____

____

____

____

/8

erreichte Punktzahl

/ 44

6 Passive voice

verstehen

Active and passive (Aktiv und Passiv)

Zahlreiche Vorgänge, Handlungen oder Zusammenhänge lassen sich entweder aktivisch oder passivisch darstellen. Der Unterschied besteht dabei lediglich in der Sichtweise bzw. in der Ausgangslage.

Aktiv
Das Aktiv wird verwendet, um auszudrücken, wer oder was etwas tut.
Anders ausgedrückt: Das Subjekt des Satzes tritt als Handelnder auf.
*John **washes** his bike every Monday.*

Passiv
Im Gegensatz zum Aktiv wird das Passiv verwendet, um auszudrücken, mit wem oder womit etwas passiert. Es geht also darum, was dem Subjekt des Satzes geschieht, und nicht, was es selbst tut.
*The car **is washed** by John every Wednesday.*

Bildung des Passiv

Wie das Aktiv kann auch das **Passiv in sämtlichen Zeitformen auftreten.** Die jeweilige Zeitform wird dabei durch die **Form von *to be*** festgelegt.

Form von *to be* + ***past participle***
*The hall is **cleaned**.*
*The people were **informed** about the new situation.*

*Simple present: Marzipan is **produced** in Lübeck.*
*Simple past: A lot of Marzipan was **produced** last month.*
*Present perfect: Marzipan has been **produced** in Lübeck since 1806.*
*Past perfect: Marzipan had been **produced** in Lübeck before.*
*Will-future: A lot more Marzipan will be **produced** in Lübeck next month.*

Verneinung und Frage
Da das Passiv mit einem Hilfsverb *(to be)* gebildet wird, kann dieses für die Verneinung und auch für die Fragestellung benutzt werden.
Verneinung: *The book wasn't bought.*
Frage: *Was the criminal caught by the police?*

Gebrauch des Passiv

Allgemein
Das Passiv wird verwendet, um auszudrücken, was mit dem Subjekt eines Satzes (Person oder Sache) geschieht.

Aus diesem Grund wird das Passiv oft bei Beschreibungen von Erfindungen (1) oder Herstellungsvorgängen (2) bzw. bei Berichten über Unfälle (3) oder Katastrophen (4) benutzt.
(1) *The telephone was* ***invented*** *by Alexander Bell.*
(2) *Cheese has always been* ***made*** *from milk.*
(3) *Two people were* ***killed*** *in a car crash last night.*
(4) *The whole area was* ***destroyed*** *by a thunder storm.*

Umwandlung von Aktiv in Passiv
Beinhaltet ein Aktivsatz ein Objekt, so kann man den Satz in aller Regel auch in einen Passivsatz umwandeln. Dabei wird das Objekt des Aktivsatzes zum Subjekt des Passivsatzes und umgekehrt.

Tausch von Subjekt und Objekt durch Verwandlung von Aktiv in Passiv – und umgekehrt.

	Subjekt	Verb		Objekt	
Aktiv	*The police*	*arrested*		*the robber*	*yesterday evening.*
Passiv	*The robber*	*was arrested*	*by*	*the police*	*yesterday evening.*

Passivsätze mit dem *by-agent*
Wenn im Aktivsatz ein spezifisches Subjekt (eines, das für die Satzaussage wichtig ist) steht bzw. wenn man erwähnen will, von wem etwas getan wird, so drückt man dies im Passiv mit *by* aus.
Aktiv: *The police* ***have caught*** *the criminal.*
Passiv: *The criminal* ***has been caught*** *by the police.*

Passiv nach modalen Hilfsverben

Genauso wie im Deutschen können Modalverben im englischen Passiv verwendet werden. Das Passiv mit einem **Modalverb** wird mit dem Infinitiv von *to be* und *past participle* des Vollverbs gebildet und sieht grammatisch so aus:

Subjekt	Modalverb	Infinitiv von *to be*	Partizip II
The computer	*can*	*be*	*used.*

Die **Zeitform** des Satzes wird durch die konjugierte Form von *to be* festgelegt.

*The hall should **be** cleaned. ⇒ simple present*

*The hall might **be being** cleaned. ⇒ present progressive*

*The hall must **have been** cleaned. ⇒ present perfect*

*The hall could **have been** being cleaned. ⇒ present perfect progressive*

Wie im normalen Passivsatz wird ein **aktives Objekt** mit *by* ausgedrückt und Adverbien nach dem ersten Verb (hier Modalverb) eingefügt.

*The work should have been completed **by** the students alone.*

Verneinungen und Fragen folgen den normalen Regeln der Zeitform.

Passiv mit Verben mit zwei Objekten

Manche englische Verben haben **zwei Objekte**, ein direktes (oft sachliches) und ein indirektes (oft persönliches) Objekt, z. B. *ask, give, tell.* Wenn Aktivsätze mit solchen Verben und zwei Objekten ins Passiv umgewandelt werden, kann entweder das direkte oder das indirekte Objekt zum Subjekt des Passivsatzes werden:

Aktiv	aktives Subjekt	Verb	indirektes Objekt	direktes Objekt
	They	*sent*	*her*	*a letter.*

Passiv

***A letter** was sent to her. **She** was sent a letter.*

Welches Objekt zum Subjekt des englischen Passivsatzes wird, hängt meist davon ab, welches besonders betont werden soll:

*A letter was sent to **Mrs Smith**, not Miss Brown!*

*She was sent **a letter**, not an e-mail!*

Wie in anderen Passivsätzen kann der *by-agent* verwendet werden:

*The politician was asked questions **by** a reporter.*

Verneinungen sowie **Fragen** folgen den normalen Regeln der Passivkonstruktion.

***Was** an expensive birthday present **promised** to him?*

***No**, he will **never** be promised an expensive birthday present.*

Test 1: Passiv (I)

üben

1 **These stories need to be reported in the newspaper.**
Make up the article titles in the *passive voice*.

Story	Title for the newspaper article
Thieves stole £1000 from a bank yesterday.	
The band has cancelled all the concerts in May.	
Someone took photos of the celebrities' secret wedding.	
The Queen will visit children in hospital.	
Somone is constantly watching the prisoners in the new jail.	
Shakespeare copied *Macbeth* from another author!	
Paparazzi were chasing Diana when she was killed.	

2 **Complete the following sentences. Use *passive forms* in the *simple past*.**

One of the most famous catastrophes in history happened on April 14, 1912 when the luxury liner "RMS Titanic" hit an iceberg and ________________ (slash open). The problem was that the iceberg ________________ (spot) too late by lookout Frederick Fleet so that the collision ________________ (cannot, avoid). Soon five of the ship's watertight compartments ________________ (flood). Passengers and some crew members ________________ (evacuate) in lifeboats. But because the crew ________________ (not train) adequately for such a disaster, many of the lifeboats ____________ only partly ________________ (fill). Most of the men ________________ (leave) on board because women and children ________________ (must, rescue) first. Two hours and forty minutes after the collision the ship broke into two halves and the people onboard ________________ (throw) into the icecold water. Almost all of them died within minutes. When the "Titanic" sank a number of distress signals ________________ (send) but no other ship was near enough to arrive in time. In the end about 1500 people (kill) and only 710 ________________ (can, rescue).

Test 2: Passiv (II)

üben

1 **Match the parts of sentences to explain how you fixed your bike yesterday.**

The punctured tyres ◇	◇ take care of your bike.
You must always ◇	◇ was fitted to the handle bars and polished.
My brother ◇	◇ were repaired by my brother.
A new bell ◇	◇ had to be oiled.
Several hours ◇	◇ helped me a lot.
The bike chain ◇	◇ were needed to complete all the jobs.

2 **Help your friend write a letter to apply *(hier: bewerben für/um)* to a new sports club. Decide whether to use the *active* or *passive voice*.**

a) ☐ I have recently named gymnast of the year at my school.
   ☐ I have recently been named gymnast of the year at my school.
b) ☐ Last year, the under-21s world championship won by my team.
   ☐ Last year, the under-21s world championship was won by my team.
c) ☐ A famous sports shop sponsors my kit *(= Ausstattung/Ausrüstung)*.
   ☐ A famous sports shop is sponsored my kit.
d) ☐ Is the equipment checked regularly by experts?
   ☐ Checked the equipment regularly by experts?
e) ☐ I understand that the equipment must put away by the athletes.
   ☐ I understand that the equipment must be put away by the athletes.

3 **You are interviewing a famous British politician. Complete his answers using the *passive*.**

Has the Queen told you secrets about the royal family?

No, I haven't been told secrets about the royal family.

a) Has someone given you a report about the destroyed sports centre in London? – Yes, …

____

____

b) Did the insurance company offer them financial help? – No, …

____

____

c) Will you give them the money to rebuild the sports centre? – Yes, ...

d) Have you promised the children new equipment? – Yes, ...

e) Will you send the centre a sports celebrity to open the new play areas? – Yes, ...

4 **Match up these phrasal verbs with their German meanings.**

to take advantage of ◊	◊ auf etwas stolz sein
to make friends with ◊	◊ verwenden
to make use of ◊	◊ ausnutzen
to pay attention to ◊	◊ aus den Augen verlieren
to lose track of ◊	◊ auf etwas achten
to take pride in ◊	◊ sich mit jemandem anfreunden

5 **Rewrite the sentences in the passive to avoid using *someone/somebody*.**

a) Someone blew the old factory up.

b) Someone was making fun of the dog's short tail.

c) Somebody took advantage of the broken fence.

Klassenarbeit Nr. 7 60 min

können

1 **Listen to the track *American Space Exploration* on the CD and answer the following questions.**

04 a) What do these abbreviations stand for? – *Wofür stehen diese Abkürzungen?*

NASA ______________________________

SETI ______________________________

/2

b) What happened in these years? Write your answers in the passive.

1958 ______________________________

____

1996 ______________________________

____

1997 ______________________________

____

2000 ______________________________

____

/4

2 **Listen again to *American Space Exploration*. True or false? Correct the false sentences.**

The EU has started a mission to Mars.

False, NASA has started a mission to Mars.

a) For four years, scientists have been trying to find life on other planets.

____

b) Water and a suitable temperature may be signs of life on a planet.

____

c) People lived on Mars billions of years ago.

____

d) Scientists listen to the radio to find signs of extraterrestrial life.

____

e) Scientists have found a star and group of planets similar to our solar system. ______________________________

____

/8

können

3 **These sentences are from the audio text about *American Space Exploration*. Rewrite them in the passive.**

a) NASA sent the "Explorer" I satellite into orbit.

____

b) Astronauts will study the ground and rocks on Mars.

____

c) Spacecrafts have taken pictures of the planet Mars.

____

d) Another programme is looking for life in other worlds.

____

/4

4 **The manager of a computer production company visits your school. Ask him questions using passive voice.**

a) when ▪ computers ▪ invent ______________________________

b) who ▪ computers ▪ invent ______________________________

c) how ▪ computers ▪ make ______________________________

d) where ▪ most ▪ computers ▪ sell ______________________________

e) what ▪ computers ▪ use for ______________________________

f) new computer ▪ develop ______________________________

/12

5 **Form either the *active* or *passive voice of* the verbs in brackets to fill in the blanks in the text.**

At the moment my parents ______________ (build) a new house near the river. About one year ago, they ______________ (go) to the bank and ______________ (give) some money to pay for the new house. The bank ______________ (agree) to lend £150,000, but £50,000 ______________ (must provide) by mum and dad. The building work ______________ (start) last January and the whole house ______________ (finish) next month. Then the inside ______________ (must decorate). I ______________ (paint) my room blue, but my sister's room ______________ (paint) in pink. We ______________ (all/be) happy when we ______________ (move in) to our new house.

/12

6 **Read the text *Our Solar System* and complete the table below.**

Our Solar System

Some of the planets in our solar system are so bright that you don't even need a telescope to see them, although they are millions of kilometers away from the Earth. So, if you look up at the sky to see the stars, you might actually see planets, too. There are nine different planets in our solar system – here are some of the most important ones:

The planet Mars is the next planet to Earth if you move away from the Sun, and it is the second-smallest planet of all in our solar system. Mars is also known as the *Red Planet* because it is bright red. Because it's further away from the Sun, it can be colder than Earth; sometimes its North and South poles, which are covered in snow, get as cold as –140 °C. On Mars, the highest recorded temperature is about 20 °C which is like a sunny day for us on Earth. Days on Mars last about one hour longer than on Earth, and years are almost twice as long as our years on Earth, as Mars takes 687 days to orbit the Sun.

The planet closest to the Sun is called Mercury, and its orbit of the Sun takes less time than Earth's. Mercury has no atmosphere, so the heat it gets from the Sun can easily escape into space. Nonetheless, the temperatures are still far hotter than on Earth, sometimes as high as 427 °C which is 61 times hotter than Earth's average temperature! But due to the lack of atmosphere and the escaping heat, it can also get very cold on Mercury. Temperatures can be as low as –173 °C, which is twice as cold as the lowest temperature we have ever had recorded on Earth.

The planet furthest away from the Sun is Neptune, which is made up of gas. The gas in Neptune's atmosphere is Methane, which also gives it its dark blue colour. On Neptune, days last 16 hours, and it has 11 moons around it. Surprisingly, although it is furthest away from the Sun, it is not the coldest, with lowest recorded temperatures of –218 °C. The planet is so far from the sun and moves so slowly that, when he first observed Neptune in 1613, Galileo thought it was a star. Neptune is 17 times the size of the Earth and needs 165 years to orbit the Sun. That means only one Neptune year has passed since it was discovered in 1846 – happy birthday Neptune!

Fill in the table with the relevant information from the text.
You will not be able to fill every square.

planet	Mars	Mercury	Neptune
highest temperature			
lowest temperature			
time taken to orbit Sun			
size			

/10

können

7 **Find the four passive sentences in the text *Our Solar System* and rewrite them using *active sentences.***

a) ____

____

b) ____

____

c) ____

____

d) ____

____

/8

8 **Write a short story in for a newspaper that fits the following headline. Write at least *eight passive sentences.***

The NASA head office has been burgled. – *In die Zentrale der NASA ist eingebrochen worden.*

____

____

____

____

____

____

____

____

____

/18

erreichte Punktzahl

/ 78

Klassenarbeit Nr. 8 60 min

können

1 **You're telling your friend about a football camp. Translate the sentences.**

a) The football shirts must be washed every week.

b) Die Spielplätze dürfen nur von Kindern benutzt werden.

c) Football could only be played between 8 a.m. and 9 p.m.

d) Wenn möglich, soll das schreckliche Essen in der Mensa (= *canteen*) vermieden (= *to avoid*) werden!

e) The final matches might have been postponed (to postpone = *verschieben*) because the weather was bad.

/10

2 **Correct your classmate or answer his questions using *passive sentences* with the words in brackets.**

a) We will give the books to another school at the end of the year. (no, next class pupils)

No, ____

b) The teachers will ask us tricky questions in the English test! (no, normal questions)

No, ____

c) Did Lucy send you a funny SMS yesterday? (no, e-mail)

No, ____

d) Have I told you a story about the ghost? (no, witch)

No, ____

e) Nike have offered the school football team a sponsorship contract! (no, hockey team)

No, ____

f) Her mother promised her a lot of sweets if she gets good grades! (no, money)

No, ____

/12

können

/6

3 **Rewrite the sentences to avoid using *someone* or *somebody*.**

a) Someone was talking about the band all day.

____

b) Somebody had washed up all the glasses.

____

c) Someone has not paid attention to the road signs.

____

4 **Read the text about dolphins and answer the questions using your own words. Try to use *passive sentences*.**

Despite their popularity, some Dolphins are still sometimes killed by humans; either for their meat or because they compete* in the ocean for the other fish. In recent years, a large example has been made of the bottlenose species of dolphin. These are often found in the sea alongside tuna fish. Fishermen can often spot dolphins more easily than the smaller tuna fish, and often surround the school of dolphins in order to catch the tuna. This often means the dolphins are caught up in the tuna fishing nets and are often killed by ruthless* commercial fishermen. *Dolphin friendly* tuna products have been launched by many supermarkets, which are made with fish that was caught using fishing methods or nets that do not harm dolphins. However, some conservation organisations and research centres have highlighted that even these methods do not keep the dolphins entirely out of danger. One such organisation is the *Whale and Dolphin Conservation Society*, which is a charity committed to improving the welfare and conservation of whales, dolphins and porpoises*. They aim to increase people's awareness of threats to the animals and where they live, to stop the killing of the animals for commercial profit, and to promote breeding of species threatened by extinction. Working together with other environmental and governmental organisations, the WDCS declared 2007 to be the (International) Year of the Dolphin, making the problem of dolphin conservation known around the world.

* to compete – *konkurrieren, im Wettbewerb stehen*; ruthless – *rücksichtslos, schonungslos, mitleidlos*; porpoise – *Tümmler*

a) Why are dolphins sometimes killed by humans?

____

____

können

b) What are *dolphin friendly* products?

____

____

b) What is the WDCS?

____

____

/6

5 True, false or not in the text?

		true	false	not in the text
a)	Dolphins are not popular.	☐	☐	☐
b)	*Dolphin friendly* fishing is perfectly safe for dolphins.	☐	☐	☐
c)	The WDCS want people to save types of dolphin from dying out.	☐	☐	☐
d)	The Year of the Dolphin is part of the Chinese calendar.	☐	☐	☐
e)	The ruthless fishermen star in commercials for tuna.	☐	☐	☐
f)	Porpoises are becoming more popular than dolphins.	☐	☐	☐
g)	The Year of the Dolphin succeeded in raising awareness.	☐	☐	☐

/7

6 Find the words in the text about dolphins that mean the same.

a) protection ______________ b) together with ______________

c) hurt ______________ d) completely ______________

e) increase ______________ f) make better ______________

/3

7 Read the description below of how British *Fish 'n' Chips* is prepared.

a) Underline all the present simple passive verbs.
b) Circle all the simple past passive verbs.

Fish 'n' chips was once called "the most British dinner". But how is it made? Well, the fresh fish is covered in batter and deep fried in oil. After the raw potatoes have been cut, they are boiled and fried as chips. British chips are much thicker than American fries. When everything is ready, the fish is served together with the chips. Sometimes it is accompanied by mushy peas or sprinkled with salt and vinegar, but this has gone out of fashion recently. In the past, fish 'n' chips was wrapped in paper and eaten with a small wooden fork. Traditionally the meal was enjoyed on a Friday evening, though tourists don't follow this rule.

/8

8 **Write a short description of how a traditional dish from your country is prepared. Write at least six *passive sentences.* (You can use the text about *Fish 'n' chips* as an example to help you.)**

___

___

___

___

___

___

___

___

/12

9 **What do you think is the most useful invention ever? Write a short text about how/where/when it was invented (if you know) and how our daily lives have been improved by it. Write at least six *passive sentences.***

___

___

___

___

___

___

___

___

/12

erreichte Punktzahl
/ 76

7 Pronouns and determiners

verstehen

Personal pronouns (Personalpronomen)

Personalpronomen können als **Subjekt** eines Satzes stehen.

	Singular	Plural
1. Person	***I*** (Ich) *love homework.*	***We*** (Wir) *hate homework.*
2. Person	***You*** (Du) *wouldn't believe this.*	***You*** (Ihr) *wouldn't believe this.*
3. Person	***He/She/It*** (Er/Sie/Es) *is late.*	***They*** (Sie) *are late.*

I (ich) wird **immer groß geschrieben**, auch wenn es nicht am Satzanfang steht.

Pronomen (Fürwörter) stehen für ein Nomen bzw. anstelle eines Nomens, Begleiter gehören zu einem Nomen und stehen vor diesem.

Personalpronomen können als **Objekt** eines Satzes stehen.

	Singular	Plural
1. Person	*John loves* ***me*** (mich).	*The teacher told* ***us*** (uns).
2. Person	*Linda will phone* ***you*** (dich).	*He asked* ***you*** (euch) *all.*
3. Person	*The company sends* ***him/her/it*** (ihn/sie/es).	*We took* ***them*** (sie).

! Im Englischen gibt es für **jede Person nur eine Objektform**:

Singular
me (mich, mir)
you (dich, dir)
him (ihn, ihm)
her (sie, ihr)
it (es, ihm)

Plural
us (uns)
you (euch)
them (sie, ihnen)

Die **Subjektform** steht **vor dem Verb**, die **Objektform** steht **nach dem Verb**.

Das deutsche Pronomen *man = jeder* kann im Englischen mit *you* oder *one* wiedergegeben werden. Für *man = Leute* wird dagegen *they* oder *people* benutzt:
Man darf hier nicht rauchen. – *You/One mustn't smoke here.*
Man sagt, Rauchen ist sehr gefährlich. – *The people/They say smoking is dangerous.*
Ein deutscher Aktivsatz mit *man* wird im Englischen meist mit Passiv wiedergegeben. *Smoking isn't allowed in public.*

Possessive pronouns (Possessivpronomen)

Possessivpronomen drücken Besitz oder Zugehörigkeit aus und **stehen anstelle eines Nomens**, das nicht wiederholt genannt werden soll.
This is your mobile phone. ***Mine*** (Meines) *is much louder.*
I can't find my key. Can I borrow ***yours*** (deinen)*?*
I'm looking for John's bag. That isn't ***his*** (seine).
Linda will miss her key. I took ***hers*** (ihre) *without noticing.*
This car is small, ***ours*** (unseres) *is much bigger.*
Linda and Sue, these earrings aren't ***yours*** (eure).
This isn't the Millers' house. ***Theirs*** (Ihres) *is on the other side of the street.*

Possessive adjectives (Possessivbegleiter)

Possessivbegleiter drücken ebenfalls Besitz oder Zugehörigkeit aus und **stehen immer vor dem Nomen, zu dem sie gehören** und das sie so näher bestimmen:
This is ***my mobile phone****, not yours.*
Can I borrow ***your key****, I can't find mine.*
John is a bit confused today so I'm looking for ***his bag****.*
Linda will be angry. I took ***her key*** *instead of mine.*
Our car *is much bigger than this one.*
Why don't you wear ***your*** *own* ***jewellery*** *instead of Mum's earrings, girls?*
The Miller family? ***Their house*** *is just on the other side of the street.*

Reflexive pronouns (Reflexivpronomen)

Viele englische Verben haben im Gegensatz zur deutschen Entsprechung **kein** Reflexivpronomen.

Das Reflexivpronomen (*reflexive pronoun*) hat **zwei Funktionen**.

1. Die wichtigste Funktion ist der **Rückbezug auf das voranstehende Subjekt des Satzes**.

I *can look after* ***myself****.*	**Ich** kann auf **mich (selbst)** aufpassen.
Can ***you*** *recognize* ***yourself*** *in the photo?*	Kannst **du dich** auf dem Photo erkennen?
John *is teaching* ***himself*** *how to cook.*	**John** bringt **sich (selbst)** das Kochen bei.
Linda *hurt* ***herself*** *yesterday.*	**Linda** hat **sich** gestern **(selbst)** verletzt.
The budgie *opened the cage* ***itself****.*	**Der Wellensittich** hat **sich** den Käfig **selbst** geöffnet.
Boys, have ***you*** *cut your hair* ***yourselves****?*	Jungs, habt **ihr euch** die Haare selbst geschnitten?
The ***girls*** *are enjoying* ***themselves*** *in the garden.*	**Die Mädchen** amüsieren **sich** im Garten.

2. Ein Reflexivpronomen kann sich aber auch auf andere Teile des Satzes zurückbeziehen, um diese besonders zu betonen. Im Deutschen verwenden wir dazu *selbst*:

*I met the **Queen herself**.*	Ich habe die Königin **selbst** (= persönlich) getroffen.
*He liked the **car itself**, but it was the wrong colour.*	Das Auto **selbst** mochte er, aber es hatte die falsche Farbe.
*I like **John himself**, but his wife is terrible.*	Ich mag John **selbst**, aber seine Frau ist furchtbar.

„Each other" / „One another" (reziproke Pronomen)

Die reziproken Pronomen (reziprok = gegenseitig, wechselseitig) *each other* und *one another* drücken aus, was sich **zwischen zwei oder mehr Personen** abspielt. In Bedeutung und Verwendung sind sie identisch und werden im Deutschen mit „gegenseitig" oder „einander" übersetzt. Beachte aber den Unterschied zwischen den reziproken und reflexiven Pronomen:

*John and Linda are looking at **each other**.*
John looks at Linda and she looks at John.

*John and Linda are looking at **themselves**.*
Both of them are looking at a picture, photo or mirror showing both of them.

Relative pronouns (Relativpronomen)

Die **Relativpronomen** *who, which, that* und *whose* leiten Relativsätze ein. Es gibt keine Unterscheidung hinsichtlich Numerus (Singular/Plural) oder grammatischem Geschlecht, wie du sie von den deutschen Relativpronomen **der, die, das** kennst, allerdings werden sie hinsichtlich der Art ihres Bezugsworts unterschiedlich verwendet:

- *who* für Personen;
- *which* für Dinge und Tiere;
- *that* für Dinge, Tiere und Personen;
- *whose* für Dinge, Tiere und Personen (entspricht dem deutschen *dessen* bzw. *deren*).

The boy who/that likes Linda is called John.
The girls who/that are talking about John are Linda and Sue.
The key which/that is missing is mine.
The keys which/that John found weren't mine.
The boy whose mother was so unfriendly is called John.
The boys whose sisters are so beautiful are called Bob and Bill.

Test 1: *Personal and possessive pronouns*

üben

1 **Put in the correct *personal pronouns*.**

John Smith is a new boy in form 7c. _______ has got a lot of questions.
Sue and Linda, some girls from his new form, are showing _______ all the important places on the school ground.
"_______ have got a few clubs in our school," says Sue. "This is where the stamp club meets every Thursday. Are _______ interested in books?
Mrs Gordon's literature club is very popular. _______ is our English teacher, _______ think _______'ve already met _______."
"And here are the sports facilities. _______ am a member of the girls hockey team, but a lot of boys play hockey, too. _______ practise every Monday afternoon."
"Can _______ tell _______ if there is a soccer team, too?"
"Oh, _______ should ask Mr Piller, the sport teacher. If _______ want to know anything about football, just ask _______." "_______ must go now. Mum is meeting _______ in town in ten minutes. But look, Jack and Robert are over there. If _______ have got any more questions, ask _______. I'm sure _______ will help _______."

2 **Robert talks about the neighbours: Put in the correct *possessive determiners.***

The Miller family lives near _______ house. There are five of them.
_______ names are Paul, Mary, Sue, Linda and Frank. Frank Miller is the youngest member. Sue and Linda are _______ sisters. Sue and Linda are twins. Frank is _______ brother, of course. John asks, "What's the name of the mother?" _______ name is Mary. Linda: "And _______ father is called Paul."

3 **Complete the dialogue with the correct *possessive pronouns* and *determiners*. Sue and Linda are not very tidy and sometimes they argue about what belongs to whom. Their mother tries to help them.**

Mrs Miller: „Look at this T-shirt. Is it _______, Linda?"

Sue: „No, it's not. It's _______. Linda always takes _______ things without asking me."

Mrs Miller: „And these shoes, are they _______, too?“

Sue: „No, they aren't, they are _______. „

Mrs Miller: „Are these Linda's CDs or _______?“

Sue: „Oh, these aren't _______ at all. We must give them back to John, they are _______.“

Mrs Miller: „And these earrings, I think I have seen them before ...“

Sue: „Sorry, Mum, they are _______.“

Mrs Miller: „Sue, if you take _______ sister's things, that is _______ business, but I want you to ask me before you take _______ things.“

4 **Translate into English.**

a) Linda und Sue bekamen viele Geschenke zu ihrem Geburtstag.

____

____

b) Linda schenkte ihrer Schwester Sue eine CD.

____

c) Sue schenkte Linda ihr Lieblingsbuch.

____

d) Linda und Sue beschenken sich immer gegenseitig an ihrem Geburtstag.

____

____

e) Alle ihre Geschenke legten sie auf einen großen Tisch.

____

____

f) Viele Freunde kamen sie besuchen und gaben ihnen Geschenke.

____

____

Test 2: *Reflexive pronouns*

1 **Put in the correct *reflexive pronoun*.**

a) Sue and Linda are old enough to look after ______________.

b) John is introducing ______________ to form 7c.

c) We are enjoying ______________ at the party.

d) Help ______________ to ice-cream, girls. I bought all your favourite flavours.

e) My mother never buys ice-cream. She makes it ______________.

f) Frank, stop fooling around and behave ______________ in class.

g) Look at my thumb. I cut ______________ when chopping onions yesterday.

2 **Translation. Decide whether you need a reflexive pronoun or not. Use your exercise book.**

a) Die Tür öffnete sich von selbst. Das muss der Wind gewesen sein.
b) Ich erinnere mich nicht, schon jemals so einen Sturm gesehen zu haben.
c) Nicht viele Leute amüsieren sich bei so einem Wetter.
d) Viele alte Leute fühlen sich nicht wohl, wenn sich das Wetter so schnell ändert.
e) Meine Oma redet dann mit sich selbst, um ruhig zu bleiben.

3 **Put in *each other/one another* or a *reflexive pronoun*.**

a) Linda fell off her bike and hurt ________________ badly.

b) In our school everyone knows ________________.

c) Go and look at ________________ in the mirror, Sue. You've got jam on your face.

d) Linda and Sue look like ________________, don't they?

e) Although Linda and Sue like ________________, they shout at ________________ nearly every day.

f) Their mother always tells ________________ to stay calm then.

Test 3: *Relative pronouns*

1 **Put in the correct *relative pronoun*.**

a) Everybody in our school has heard about the boy ___________ mobile phone was confiscated last Monday.

b) The boy, ___________ has got twin sisters, is called Frank Miller.

c) The boy ___________ twin sisters are called Sue and Linda is in my form.

d) The bell ___________ sound could be heard in class is Big Ben.

e) The mobile phone ___________ disrupted class with the sound of Big Ben belongs to Frank Miller.

f) The mobile phone ___________ sound disrupted class was confiscated by the headmaster.

g) I need a mobile phone ___________ doesn't make a sound at all.

h) The parents ___________ son got into trouble had to talk to the headmaster.

i) The discussion, ___________ lasted about ten minutes, was not very pleasant.

j) The headmaster is a man ___________ always insists on keeping the school rules.

2 **Linda shows Frank some photos. Make *relative clauses*.**

This is my cousin Joe. His mother came from Australia.

This is my cousin Joe whose mother came from Australia.

a) This is Aunt Jessica. Her family emigrated to Australia 200 years ago.

____

b) This is Uncle Robert. He married Aunt Jessica twenty years ago.

____

c) This is a part of the Australian outback. It has some very dangerous snakes.

____

d) This is a beautiful house. They bought it for their children.

____

e) This is my first boyfriend. His name was Sean.

____

Klassenarbeit Nr. 9 45 min

können

1 **Translate.**

a) Um die Umwelt zu schützen, sollte man öfter sein Fahrrad benutzen.

____

____

b) Man weiß ja auch, dass Radfahren einem guttut.

____

c) Wenn man weniger mit seinem Auto fährt, spart man auch Geld.

____

/6

2 **Put in a *reflexive pronoun* or *each other/one another*.**

a) Sue and Linda talk to ______________ about everything.

b) They know ______________ like nobody else.

c) Sue and Linda are looking at ______________ in the bathroom mirror.

d) The sisters help ______________ with their hair styles.

e) They always talk to ______________ before they get a new haircut.

f) But they never do these haircuts ______________.

/6

3 **Connect the sentences using *relative pronouns*.**
You might need to change some words.

a) Is this John Miller? Did this pupil get into trouble last Monday?

____

b) Here is his mobile phone. Its sound disrupted class.

____

c) These are our school rules. They say mobile phones mustn't be used in class.

____

d) Mr Finch is John's form teacher. He took John's mobile phone away.

____

e) Mr Gill is very angry. He is the headmaster.

____

/10

4 **Put in *reflexive pronouns* or *each other* where necessary.**

a) "I can take care of ____________, Mum," Linda said as she went on the bus to Devon.

b) "Well, enjoy ____________ and call us when you arrive," Linda's mother answered.

c) "I will, Mum. John, Sue and I will certainly enjoy ____________ at the festival, it's always great fun!"

d) On the bus Linda and Sue were so excited they started singing to ____________.

e) John and the girls met in Exeter. They kissed ____________ and then John said: "I've booked us the same lovely rooms in the hostel we had last year. We are really lucky this year!"

f) When they got to the hostel, Linda didn't remember the bump in the stairs and hurt ____________ when she stumbled and fell.

g) But it wasn't too bad and some time later she was able to move again and laugh about ____________.

/8

5 **Translate.**

a) John und Jenny waren sehr überrascht, als sie sich im Zug zum Festival trafen.

____

____

b) Sie sahen sich durch das Fenster im Abteil an und lächelten sich zu.

____

____

c) Jennys Freund sah sie durchs Fenster von außen, als sie sich nebeneinander setzten.

____

____

d) Er ärgerte sich, weil er nicht selbst zum Festival mitkommen konnte.

____

____

/8

6 **Put in the correct *pronouns* and *determiners*.**

A Man of Many Wives

Henry VIII was King of England from 1509 until _________ death. Henry VIII was the second son of Henry VII and Elizabeth of York and only became king because _________ elder son Arthur died in 1502. Henry VIII is well-known because _________ was married to six different women: Catherine of Aragon, Anne Boleyn, Jane Seymor, Anne of Cleves, Katherine Howard, and Catherine Parr. During _________ reign as king many important laws were made. Henry named _________ as supreme Head of the Church of England, and used _________ new position to get divorced from _________ first wife, Catherine of Aragon. The lives of _________ six wives can be summarized as follows: divorced, beheaded, died, divorced, beheaded, survived. Catherine Parr survived, as _________ husband died before _________ did. Anne of Cleves also outlived _________, after _________ divorce. Three of _________ six wives bore Henry children who survived _________ childhood and all of _________ ruled England: Edward VI, Mary I and Elizabeth I.

/15

erreichte Punktzahl

/ 53

8 Adverb and adjective

Adjective

Adjektive drücken Eigenschaften oder Merkmale des Substantivs oder Pronomens aus, zu dem sie gehören.

Ein Adjektiv kann unmittelbar vor seinem **Bezugssubstantiv** stehen:
*I have got a green **car**. She is a beautiful **girl**. He has got funny **friends**.*

Ein Adjektiv kann auch nach dem Verb *be* stehen und sich auf ein Substantiv oder Pronomen zurückbeziehen:
*My car is **green**. She is so **beautiful**. They are **funny**.*

Steigerung

Adjektive können gesteigert werden, das heißt, es gibt neben ihrer Grundform (Positiv) eine Vergleichsform (Komparativ) und eine höchste Steigerungsform (Superlativ). Unterschieden werden drei Steigerungsmuster.

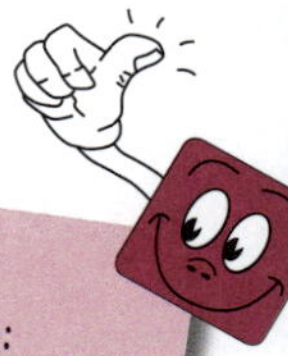

Schreibregeln:
- Stummes -e fällt weg:
  nice - nicer - nicest,
  fine - finer - finest.
- Endkonsonant wird nach einfachem, kurzen und betonten Vokal verdoppelt:
  big - bigger - biggest.
- -y nach Konsonant wird zu -i:
  funny - funnier - funniest.

1. **Steigerung mit *-er* und *-est***
   - einsilbige bzw. einsilbig gesprochene Adjektive:
     great – greater – greatest
     nice – nicer – nicest
     fast – faster – fastest
   - zweisilbige bzw. zweisilbig gesprochene Adjektive:
     quiet – quieter – quietest
   - zweisilbige bzw. zweisilbig gesprochene Adjektive, deren 2. Silbe sehr kurz gesprochen wird, die also auf *-le, -er, -ow, -y* enden:
     simple – simpler – simplest; clever – cleverer – cleverest
     narrow – narrower – narrowest; happy – happier – happiest
2. **Steigerung mit *more* und *most***
   - Alle zweisilbigen Adjektive, die sich nicht auf *-er* und *-est* steigern lassen:
     famous – more famous – most famous
     difficult – more difficult – most difficult
   - Adjektive mit drei und mehr Silben:
     fantastic – more fantastic – most fantastic
     expensive – more expensive – most expensive
3. **unregelmäßige Steigerungsformen**
   - *good – better – best*
   - *bad – worse – worst*
   - *much/many – more – most*
   - *little – less – least*

Vergleiche

Im Englischen kann man Vergleiche ebenso wie im Deutschen auf drei Weisen formulieren:

1. Mit **(not) as … as** [(nicht) so …wie] in Verbindung mit der Grundform des Adjektivs.
   *My hair is **not as** long **as** your hair.*
   *This car is **as** expensive **as** that one over there.*
2. Mit der Kombination der **Komparativform** des Adjektivs **plus *than***.
   *My hair is **longer than** your hair.*
   *This car is **more expensive than** that one over there.*
3. Mit der Kombination ***the* + Superlativ** des Adjektivs.
   *Your hair is **the longest**.*
   *This car is the **most expensive one** in the shop.*

Personalpronomen nach than und as stehen meist in der Objektform: John is stronger than me/him/her…

Adverb

Adverbs of manner (Adverbien der Art und Weise)

Mit Adverbien der Art und Weise drücken wir aus, wie – also auf welche Weise – etwas geschieht.

Tom drove nervously. → Wie fuhr Tom? – Nervös.

Bildung der Adverbien

Die meisten Adverbien bilden wir, indem wir an ein Adjektiv die Endung ***-ly*** anhängen (z. B. *nervous**ly**, quick**ly**, slow**ly**, sad**ly**, quiet**ly*** etc.).

Bei der Schreibung von Adverbien die auf ***-ly*** enden, gibt es eine Reihe von Besonderheiten:

	Adjektiv	Adverb
y wird vor *-ly* zu *i*:	*happ**y***	*happ**ily***
nach der Endung *-ic* hängt man *ally* an:	*fantast**ic***	*fantasti**cally***
die Endung *-le* fällt vor *-ly* weg:	*simp**le***	*simp**ly***

Achtung Ausnahme!
public (Adjektiv) - publicly (Adverb)

Sonderformen

	Adjektiv	Adverb
völlig neue Form:	*good*	*well*
identische Formen:	*far*	*far*
	fast	*fast*
	hard	*hard*
bei der Adjektivendung *ly* verwenden wir für das Adverb die Umschreibung *in a … way*.	*friendly*	*in a friendly way*
	lovely	*in a lovely way*

auch bei den Adjektiven free, high, late, left, long, near, right, wrong haben die Adverbien genau die gleiche Form.

Adverbs of time (Adverbien der Zeit)

Mit Adverbien der Zeit drücken wir aus, **wann etwas geschieht**. Sie haben keine besondere Endung, da es für sie keine entsprechenden Adjektive gibt (z. B. ***already, late, soon, afterwards, now, just, still***).

I am leaving ***now****. I will go home* ***soon****.*

Adverbs of place (Adverbien des Ortes)

Mit Adverbien des Ortes drücken wir aus, **wo etwas geschieht**. Sie haben keine besondere Endung, da es für sie keine entsprechenden Adjektive gibt (z. B. ***abroad, anywhere, here, outside, somewhere, there, underground***).

Tom and Linda are playing ***outside****. My mobile is* ***here*** *in my rucksack.*

Steigerung von Adverbien

Auch Adverbien können gesteigert werden, die drei möglichen Steigerungsmuster sind mit denen des Adjektivs weitgehend identisch.

1. **Steigerung mit *-er* und *-est***
   Einsilbige Adverbien und *early*: *soon – sooner – soonest; early – earlier – earliest.* Es gelten die gleichen Besonderheiten bei der Schreibung wie bei den Adjektiven, die nach diesem Muster gesteigert werden.
2. **Steigerung mit *more* und *most***
   – Adverbien, die auf *-ly* enden (außer *early*).
   extremely – more extremely – most extremely;
   carefully – more carefully – most carefully
   – Andere mehrsilbige Adverbien:
   often – more often – most often
3. **unregelmäßige Steigerungsformen**
   – *well – better – best* *badly – worse – worst*
   – *much – more – most* *little – less – least*

Adverb oder Adjektiv nach bestimmten Verben

Für die Beschreibung der Art und Weise, wie eine Tätigkeit oder Handlung ausgeführt wird, muss ein Adverb verwendet werden.

*Tom shouts **angrily**. Tina sings **well**.*
*John screams **terribly**.*

Einige Verben beschreiben jedoch keine Tätigkeiten, sondern Zustände oder Eigenschaften (sogenannte Zustandsverben, diese können auch keine *-ing*-Form bilden, → Seite 7). Nach solchen Verben stehen immer Adjektive, keine Adverbien.

*Tom looks **angry**. Tina sounds **good**.*

Vergleiche

Adverbien können nach den gleichen Mustern wie Adjektive verglichen werden:

1. mit *(not) as …as*: *She does not/She sing(s) as well as I do.*
2. mit Komparativ + *than*: *She sings better than I do.*
3. mit Superlativ: *She sings best.*

Stellung der Adverbien und adverbiale Bestimmungen

Es gibt vier Positionen, an denen Adverbien und adverbiale Bestimmungen im Satz stehen können:

1. Vor dem Subjekt *(front position)* stehen meist sogenannte **Satzadverbien** (Of course, maybe, suddenly, unfortunately, then, at first), z. B.: *Maybe the bus is late. Suddenly the weather changed.*
2. Zwischen Subjekt und Vollverb bzw. nach dem ersten Hilfsverb (*mid-position*) stehen häufig **Adverbien der unbestimmten Zeit oder Häufigkeit**, z. B.: *The bus has often been late. The weather has never before changed that quickly.*
3. Nach dem Vollverb bzw. nach dem Objekt (*end-position*) stehen normalerweise die **Adverbien der Art und Weise** (*carefully, well, badly, quickly,* z. B.: *The weather has never before changed that quickly.*), die **Adverbien der Zeit** (*yesterday, now, in 2015*, z. B.: *The holidays end next week.*) sowie die **Adverbien des Ortes** (*here, there, to London*, z. B.: *We visited my uncle in Berlin.*)
4. **Gradadverbien** (*very, quite, nearly, too, fairly, really*) stehen unmittelbar vor dem Verb (bzw. Verbpartikel), das sie verstärken bzw. abschwächen: *I was quite nervous. I talked too fast.*

Test 1: Adjective and adverb: Form

1 Comparisons. Put in the missing form of the adjective.

a) Linda and Sue are twins, but Linda is ____________ (pretty) than Sue.
Yes, but Sue is the ____________ (clever) of the two.

b) I got the ____________ (good) mark in today's test. But it was the ____________ (easy) test we have had this year.
Last week's test was much ____________ (difficult).

c) Can I have ____________ (much) champagne, please?
No, you can't. You have had the ____________ (much) already.
That is not true. I have had ____________ (little) than you.

d) Which is the ____________ (big) town in Europe? I don't know, but Munich is certainly the ____________ (interesting) and ____________ (safe) than most other big towns in the world.

e) Our new form teacher is much ____________ (nice) than our old one.
Yes, but the old one was one of the ____________ (strict) teachers I have ever met.

2 Make adverbs from the following adjectives.

a) slow	____________	b) easy	____________
c) fast	____________	d) careful	____________
e) hard	____________	f) bad	____________
g) terrible	____________	h) unfortunate	____________
i) high	____________	j) good	____________

3 Translate into English. Use your exercise book.

a) Ein Mercedes ist nicht so elegant wie ein Rolls Royce.
b) Ja, aber ein Rolls Royce ist auch viel teurer als ein Mercedes.
c) Die schnellsten und schönsten Autos werden von Porsche gebaut.
d) Ein Ford ist nicht so schnell, aber auch viel billiger.
e) Mein Auto ist das schlechteste, das man haben kann.

Test 2: Adjective and adverb: Use

1 **Choose the correct adjective from the list, form the adverb and complete the sentences.**

angry ▪ bad ▪ beautiful ▪ careful ▪ extreme ▪ fast ▪ fair ▪ good ▪ hard ▪ easy ▪ quiet

Linda has to do her homework again because it was done ____________.

Sue didn't have to do hers again because she did it ever so ____________.

But Linda had done her homework very ____________ because she doesn't like to work ____________. Now she is sitting in her room ____________, writing ____________ in her best handwriting. She knows that this time she must work ____________ or her teacher will shout at her ____________ tomorrow. Linda thinks she is not treated ____________ because Sue always gets on ____________ with all her teachers because she can be ____________ polite.

2 **Underline all the adjectives in the text in red and all the adverbs in black.**

Linda's exercise book is full of mistakes – extremely full, it has never been as bad as this year. Most of these mistakes only happen because Linda is not doing her work carefully. Her head is always in the clouds the clouds and what she likes best is dreaming about her lovely boyfriend John. Her sister Sue is very angry with Linda because she hates being told off by the teacher – especially since Sue always does her homework ever so carefully. But Mrs Brown sometimes still confuses the twins and then Sue doesn't think it is funny to be punished for what her lazy sister does wrong.

3 **Decide whether you need the *adverb* or *adjective* to complete the sentences. Cross out the wrong one.**

a) "Why are you so sad ▪ sadly, Linda?"
b) "I think Miss Brown has really treated me bad ▪ badly."
c) "Why, what terrible ▪ terribly things did she do?"
d) "Well, usual ▪ usually she is very nice ▪ nicely, but yesterday she made me feel uncomfortable ▪ uncomfortably because of my homework."
e) "What was wrong ▪ wrongly with it?"
f) "I had done it quite hasty ▪ hastily because I came home hungry ▪ hungrily and she said I was just too lazy ▪ lazily to care about my work."

Test 2: *Adjective and adverb: Use*

4 **Rewrite the sentences using *adverbs* and the verb in brackets without changing its meaning.**

I am a slow swimmer.

I swim slowly.

a) Linda is a good singer (to sing).

___

b) Sue is a careful listener (to listen).

___

c) John is a bad football player (to play football).

___

d) I am a fast driver (to drive).

___

e) We are fair players (to play).

___

5 **Where does the adverb have to go? Mark with an x.**

a) Linda works at the weekend. (always)

b) She gets home before six in the evening. (never)

c) Linda and Sue go to the cinema. (often)

d) Linda is very tired. She sleeps enough. (hardly)

e) She has one free day per week. (only)

6 **Listen to the track *Los Angeles* on the CD. Then write from dictation.**

05

Klassenarbeit Nr. 10 45 min

können

1 **Underline the *adverbs* and *adverbial phrases* in the text on Rugby in Wales. Then decide what type of adverb they are and group them in the categories.**

For many people Wales is closely connected to Rugby because it is a very popular game there. In 1999 the Rugby World Cup Final Tournament was held in Cardiff's National Stadium, attracting fans from all over the world. The first Rugby World Cup Tournament was in 1987 and is repeated every four years. Rugby is thought to have originated when a boy at Rugby School in England picked up and carried the ball carefully during a game of football in 1823. Then the game of rugby became quite popular in other English schools and even today it is often the most popular game among male students .

Satzadverbien: ______________________________

Adverbien der unbestimmten Zeit/Häufigkeit: ______________________________

Adverbien der Art und Weise: ______________________________

Adverbien des Ortes: ______________________________

____

____

Adverbien der Zeit: ______________________________

____

Adverbien des Grades: ______________________________

____

/30

2 **Complete the table with the missing forms.**

adjective	adverb	comparative	superlative
good			
much			
	fast		
		bigger	
			loudest
		funnier	
	near		
			least
		more useful	
terrible			

/30

können

3 **Find and correct the mistakes.**

There is no better country for a bike tour than Wales. You can easy keep away from big roads and enjoy the beautifully landscape. There are many lanes with few cars. It's a cyclist's paradise really!
There are of course not only famous national parks like Snowdonia, Pembrokeshire Coast, and Brecon Beacons which are always perfectly for a bike tour, but the normal places with their beautiful scenery are attractive often.
You'll see maybe not only great rivers, but beavers, salmon and other wildlife animals often here appear.

/11

4 **Decide whether you need the *adverb* or the *adjective* to complete the sentence. Cross out the wrong one.**

All about Wales
Wales is situated in the sunny ▪ sunnily south-west of Great Britain.
To the west and north of Wales is the Irish Sea and ferries run regular ▪ regularly across to Cork from Swansea, which is Wales' second-largest city.
Since the 1800s Wales has been a successful ▪ successfully industrial state and still exports a lot of coal and steel. However, many factories and mines were closed down in the 1980s and the service industry became more successful ▪ successfully.
Most of the Welsh population lives quiet ▪ quietly in the valleys and the coastal areas of South Wales. Other areas, in Mid Wales, the south west and west are main ▪ mainly hilly countryside areas. The capital city of Wales, Cardiff, is also in the south. In this area English is the most common ▪ commonly used language, although a separate Welsh language exists and all official documents and road-signs are bilingual.
A separate parliament for Wales, the *National Assembly*, was formed in 1999, and has limited power to pass laws independent ▪ independently of the main U.K. Parliament in London.
The Welsh people like to preserve their cultural identity. They wear traditional/traditionally dress and eat traditional ▪ traditionally foods, such as Welsh cakes, rye bread, faggots, Welsh rarebit (cheese on toast) and corned-beef pasties.
Wales is also famous/famously for choirs, sheep, rugby, whisky and mountain trekking, it is a good ▪ well destination for your family holiday!

/12

erreichte Punktzahl

/ 83

Kapitel 1: *Present tense/past tense*

Test 1: *Simple present/ present progressive* Seite 10 – 12

1 Every Wednesday John and Jill drive to London to go shopping. They don't want to use the bus because it is always very crowded. Sometimes John's little brother Tom goes with them.
He doesn't have much pocket money so he only wants to have some fun in the big city. All three of them love the many famous sights and always try to visit at least one.

2 a) Where do you come from?
b) Where do you live?
c) Which subjects do you like?
d) What are your hobbies?
e) Have you got a brother or sister?
(*have* ist selbst Hilfsverb, daher keine *to do* Umschreibung)
Auch möglich: *Do you have a brother/ sister?* (Amerikanisches Englisch)

3 Einige Verben weisen Besonderheiten bei der Schreibung auf:
a) sit – sitting
b) wait – waiting
c) walk – walking
d) hope – hoping
e) put – putting
f) try – trying

4 a) I'm playing in my room.
b) The pupils aren't listening.
c) Are they playing football?
d) Jane is making the beds.
e) (At the moment) he's talking to Sarah.

5 Tom: "Hi, Linda. This is Tom. What are you doing at the moment? " Linda: "I 'm watching Star Wars – Episode V. I love it. I think it's the best Star Wars film."
Tom: "Oh, yes. I like it, too. Would you like to go swimmming after the film?"
Linda: "That sounds great, but Sarah is also here and she doesn't like swimming very much. But why don't you come and watch Star Wars with us?"
Tom: "Well, the problem is that I 'm tidying up my room at the moment. I always have to tidy up my room on Mondays."
Linda: "Ok, you can come later. We want to watch Episode VI as well."
Tom: "Hm, Episode VI isn't my favourite Star Wars film ..."
Linda: "Oh, Jane is coming home now. Maybe she wants to go swimming with you? Wait a moment ..."
Tom: "Ok. And does she want to go?"
Jane: "Hi, Tom. Swimming is great. Let's meet at the swimming pool in about 30 minutes."
Tom: "Great, see you there."

Test 2: *simple present/ present progressive* Seite 13

1 Neben der Situation *(What they are doing* ***now****)* bestimmen Signalwörter, welche Zeitform verlangt wird.
a) Is John watching TV? No, he isn't.
He is reading comics. He never watches TV before eight o'clock.
b) Are you doing your homework? Yes, I am. I always do my homework after school.
c) Where is Dave going? He is going to the cinema. He goes every Thursday.
d) Why are you leaving so early? I usually try to catch the last train home.
e) Are the pupils listening to their teacher at the moment? Yes, of course. They always listen carefully.

2 Beispiellösung
Dear John,
I hope you're fine. We are having our summer vacation at the moment, which is great. Usually I try to stay up late and sleep until 9 or 10 in the morning. In the evenings I go out with my friends or watch a DVD. We love to go to the cinema as well. In the afternoons we often go swimming. There is a nice lake not far away from our house so that we can cycle. At the moment I'm working on a model car. It's an Aston Martin DB5, an exact replica of the famous Bond car from „Goldfinger". It's pretty hard work because of the many details but it's also a lot of fun. Oh, my mum is coming. I'm sure she wants me to do the washing-up.
Please write soon and tell me something about your holidays. I hope the weather in California is as nice as here in Germany.
Yours Tom

Test 3: *simple past/ past progressive* Seite 14 – 16

1 I went to the cinema yesterday. Two of my friends came with me. We went into town by bike. I wore a helmet, but one of my friends did not. I knew it was a long film, so I took my bike lights with me, too. Again, one of my friends' bike had no lights. When we arrived at the cinema, we looked at the posters first. Yes, there they were: The posters said the cinema was still showing the film. We bought the tickets and ran inside quickly. Yes, we caught the best seats

in the middle! We enjoyed the film very much. When we rode home on our bikes it was already dark. I put on my lights and my helmet, which my friends made a lot of jokes about. I became angry and rode my bike as fast as I could. But then! My friend Nick wanted to have some more fun. Toward a sharp bend he overtook my bike and then he braked suddenly in front of me.
Of course I crashed into him. I shouted at him angrily before I fell off my bike into the mud. My head hit the ground hard, but luckily I had my helmet on which protected me. My friends never told jokes about my *silly hat* again.

2 a) Where did you go yesterday?
b) Who went with you?
c) How did you get into town?
d) What did you do first?
e) Why did you run inside quickly?
f) Did you enjoy the film?

3 a) Our teacher Mr Miller wanted to know what the pupils were doing last Saturday.
b) Robby said he was practising the guitar all day.
c) Anna said she was visiting her grandparents in Wales.
d) John and Jack answered they were cycling to Bradford.
e) David said he was painting his room.
f) Elizabeth said she was moving house.
g) Diana reported she was running her first marathon.

4 Mr Miller: „What were you doing last Saturday, Robby?"
Robby: „I was playing the guitar."
Mr Miller: „Were you playing the guitar, too, Anna?"
Anna: „No, I wasn't. I was visiting/visited my grandparents. We went to their local cinema because they wanted to see the new Bond movie."
Mr Miller: „Oh, really? Did you like it?"
Anna: „Yes, it was great. My grandparents loved it, too."

5 **A trip to NYC**
Last August, the Millers flew to New York. When they arrived at JFK it was raining heavily. Fortunately they could find a taxi which brought them to their hotel.
The following morning the weather was great again and the sun was shining.
So they took a ferry to Liberty Island because John wanted to see the Statue of Liberty. The trip was fantastic and they had a wonderful view of the Manhattan skyline. But John's sister Sally is more into shopping, so they walked down Fifth Avenue in the afternoon. Of course she didn't buy anything because it's one of the world's most for expensive places.
While Sally and her mother were looking for extravagant clothing stores like Prada, John and his dad went to the famous toy store FOA Schwartz. On their second day the Millers visited some very interesting museums and had a picknick at Central Park.
The following days they often used the New York Subway and saw many other famous sights like the Brooklyn Bridge, Wall Street or Grand Central Station. Of course they also went up the Empire State Building.
They had to wait more than an hour but it was worth it. While they were looking at all the skyscrapers from above, the sun went down/was going down and bathed the whole scenery in a wonderful red light. That surely was one of the greatest moments of their trip.

Klassenarbeit Nr. 1 — Seite 17–19

Falls nicht anders angegeben, gibt es für jede Teilaufgabe bzw. jeden Teilschritt einen Punkt.

1 Signalwörter für das *simple past* sind grau, die für das *past progressive* sind hellrot, Zustandsverben rot hinterlegt.
Last week Paul went on a school trip to Stonehenge. The pupils slept in tents and in the evening they made a big fire, sat around it and sang songs. Then some boys wanted to listen to scary stories, so they asked their teacher to tell one. Mr Miller thought for a while and then he told this old story: Many years ago there were two poor old people and their only son. The boy was always hungry and he was eating all the time. So he grew fatter and fatter. Because he needed so much food and also new clothes every month, his parents were getting poorer and poorer. One night he looked at the moon. It always grew and then decreased in size again and then it all started again from the beginning. He then very much wished to be like the moon, so he could grow fat without having to buy new clothes all the time. In the morning he was gone, but the next night two fat full moons were shining among the stars.
Of course, the boys didn't believe a word of this and they all went to sleep inside their tents.

2 Dear Debbie,
How are you? I am having a great time at the moment because my parents went on

holiday last Saturday and I am staying at my aunt's house. We did a lot of fun things last weekend, and we are laughing at my uncle's jokes all the time. Last Monday I told my aunt about Alton Towers. She wanted to know everything about the attractions and then we went there last Tuesday. It was fantastic! On Wednesday I tried to phone you but you weren't at home. I wanted to ask you about next weekend because I want to visit you over the weekend. What are your plans? We had a great time together last time! Please phone me soon!
From, Sita

3 a) John came home while we were watching TV.
b) The doorbell rang while Jane was doing her homework
c) They saw an accident while they they were cycling.
d) I heard a strange noise while I was reading the newspaper.

4 a) Tom was waiting for me when I arrived at the station.
b) "What were you doing at this time last Monday?"
"I was asleep."
c) "Did you go out last night?"
"No, I was too tired."
d) "How fast were you driving when the accident happened?"
e) John took a photograph of her while she wasn't looking.
f) I was walking along the street when I suddenly heard footsteps behind me. Somebody was following me.
g) Yesterday evening I dropped a plate when I was doing the washing up. Fortunately it didn't break.

5 a) He had a huge appetite for life and power and he led England into a new age.
b) As a young man Henry was very attractive and strong and he spent his father's money on foreign adventures.
c) The first reason was need for money, the second reason was that he needed a son who could follow him to the throne.
d) Because of the conflict the national State Church was established. / Because of the conflict Henry established the national State Church.

Je 2 Punkte

68–55 Punkte	54–34 Punkte	33–0 Punkte
Super!	In Ordnung!	Bitte noch einmal üben!

Kapitel 2: *Present perfect, past perfect, future*

Test 1: *Present perfect/ simple past* — Seite 25

1 Signalwörter für das *present perfect* sind grau, Signalwörter für *simple past* sind rot hinterlegt.
We have lived in England for almost a year and during that time we have learnt a lot about England and its people. We have been to nice pubs and we have eaten fish and chips, which is really delicious. Last Christmas we even tried Christmas pudding. We have visited a number of famous sights and have travelled to beautiful towns, but we haven't met the Queen yet. We have enjoyed our time here but we have not found a good job anywhere. So last week we decided that we will move back to Germany.

2 Tom: "Have you ever been to England?"
Sarah: "Yes, I lived there there for almost a year."
Tom: "And have you met the Queen?"
Sarah: "No, unfortunately I haven't met the Queen."
Tom: "When did you return to Germany?"
Sarah: "We returned to Germany a week ago."
Tom: "Why did you come back?"
Sarah: "Well, it's because I couldn't find a good job anywhere."

Test 2: *Present perfect progressive* — Seite 26–28

1 a) What have you been doing all day?
b) I have been working in the garden all morning.
c) My mother has been reading this new book for weeks.
d) John has been playing computer games all the time.
e) My father has been working on a model spaceship for days.
f) Anna has been revising vocabulary since breakfast.
g) Our dog has been jumping around in the garden for two hours.
h) Aunt Audrey has been watching TV for hours.
i) We have just been talking about what you have been doing all day.

2 John has done his homework quickly. He is finished now. But Jack has wasted a lot of time, because he has been watching TV all afternoon. John has just phoned his friend Peter and they have been discussing plans for the evening since then. Meanwhile Jack has been working rapidly on his homework to catch up with his brother.

3 a) I have been living in this town since 1995.
b) I have never worked with this book.
c) Have you ever been to the USA?
d) Tom has just arrived at the station.
e) He has never run a marathon.
f) I can't buy this CD because I have already spent all my money.
g) We haven't decided yet what we want to do.
h) Haven't you done your homework yet?
i) They have been playing football for three hours.

4 Model answer
Hi David,
A lot has happened since your last mail. We had a really difficult English test at school but because of our many telephone conversations and e-mails I had no problems with it. My sister has passed her final exams so that she can go to university now. She has been revising day and night and so she's quite exhausted now. Well, I think that's enough about school.
Last week I saw the new Bond-film at our local cinema. Have you already seen it? I think it's great. It has been the most entertaining movie since last year's Mission: Impossible 3.
By the way what have you been doing since our last contact? I hope you had a great time. I'm looking forward to your answer.
Yours, Peter

Test 3: *Past perfect/ past progressive* — Seite 29–31

1 a) The Romans had played an important role in British history.
b) How had they reached the British Isles?
Vorsicht: keine *to-do*-Umschreibung
c) The Romans had come to Britain by ship.
d) What had the Romans done in Britain?
Vorsicht: keine *to-do*-Umschreibung, aber *do* ist hier Vollverb.
e) They had beaten the Celts in most battles, but they hadn't conquered the whole country.
Vorsicht: keine *to-do*-Umschreibung bei der Verneinung im *past perfect*
f) Had the Romans learned the Celtic language?
Vorsicht: keine *to-do*-Umschreibung
g) They hadn't learned the Celtic language but had spoken Latin.
Vorsicht: keine *to-do*-Umschreibung
h) Had the Romans founded important cities in Britain?
Vorsicht: keine *to-do*-Umschreibung
i) The teacher hadn't said anything about cities but he had said they had built a lot of important roads.
Vorsicht: keine *to-do*-Umschreibung

2 The Celts came to Britain 2500 years ago. Some of them lived/had lived in Western Europe, others stayed/had stayed in Central Europe before they began to settle in Britain. The Celts had been living in Britain for about six centuries before the Romans arrived. Because the Romans had beaten the Celts in lots of battles, the Celts had to get along with the Romans. The Celts already had settled there for more than 1000 years before the Angles and Saxons came to Britain. Before they went to the British Isles, they lived/had lived in what is today Denmark and northern Germany. Because the Celts had lost battles against the Angles and Saxons, they moved west to the hills of Cornwall, Scotland and Wales.

3 a) Though the Celts had been terrible warriors the Romans didn't fear them.
b) After the Romans had conquered big parts of England, many of them married Celtic women.
c) There were almost no Roman influences in Scotland as they hadn't got across Hadrian's Wall.
d) Although the Romans had been successful, the Celts didn't learn their language.

Klassenarbeit Nr. 2 — Seite 32–33

Falls nicht anders angegeben, gibt es für jede Teilaufgabe bzw. jeden Teilschritt einen Punkt.

1 Darren has always wanted to spend a holiday at an adventure camp, and now he has been at Brecon Beacon weight loss camp for almost a week. He has been doing lots of activities and he has met some nice people. He even says he has enjoyed most of the time at the camp. Yesterday, all the kids sat around a camp fire. Darren was talking to Liz all evening. He has known her since last Saturday, but everybody could see that he liked her very much. On Monday Darren learnt a lot about cooking healthy meals and he found out that he could even like it. This was a new experience for a boy who has eaten only junk food or has put TV dinners into the microwave all his life. There have been a lot more things for him to learn since he came to the camp. For example, walking up and down the hills for more than three hours was an experience his feet won't forget so quickly ... Darren has planned/plans to do more sport, but it will take a long time before he can wear t-shirts a normal size.

2 a) Since 1999 seven weight-loss camps have opened in the UK.
b) Darren has not done any sport since he has weighed more than 100 kg.
c) The teenagers at the camp have been playing rugby for one hour everyday since the day they arrived.
d) Darren has lost 7 kg since the day he came to the camp.
e) He has not eaten any chips for six weeks.

31–26 Punkte	25–16 Punkte	15–0 Punkte
Super!	In Ordnung!	Bitte noch einmal üben!

Kapitel 3: *Future*

Test 1: *Will-future* — Seite 36

1 **Taurus** (between April 21 and May 21): You won't like your family's plans for the weekend, but nobody will ask your opinion. You will meet someone nice at a party, but he/she will be very shy. Sunday won't be very exciting, a good opportunity to relax! **Gemini** (between May 21 and June 21): You will hear some news you won't believe at first, but you will realize it is the bitter truth. An old friend you have always trusted will have the unpleasant duty of revealing the secret to you. Your life will change dramatically on Sunday!

2 John: "Martin is in our football team. Will you come (you, come) with me to his match tomorrow afternoon?"
Dave: "No, I won't come. I'm more into tennis."
John: "Oh, come on. It's Martin's first big match. We must cheer him. And I'm sure it will be a lot of fun."
Dave: "By the way, when will it start?"
John: "I think it will begin at 3 o'clock."
Dave: "Well, there's a problem. Every Thursday I have piano lessons at four. My parents won't be happy if I miss one of them."
John: "Ok, you could only watch the first half."
Dave: "Ok then. But you will have to pick me up. I don't know the way to the stadium."
John: "No problem. I will pick you up half an hour before the match.
See you tomorrow. I'm sure you won't regret it."

Test 2: *Going-to-future* — Seite 37

1 a) Is Jack going to buy some ice-cream?
b) Linda isn't going to watch the basketball match.
c) What are you going to do next weekend?
d) Jake and Tom are going to join the chess club.
e) My father is going to sell his car.
f) When are they going to fly to Italy?
g) I am going to repair my motorbike.
h) This year we aren't going to visit our relatives in England.

2 a) My father is going to wash his car this afternoon.
b) My mother is going to tidy up the garage tomorrow. I have no plans to help her.
c) When will your brother tidy up the garden?
d) Are we going to have/Will we have a garden party? Yes, we are/will.
e) Then I will bake some cookies.

Test 3: *Going-to-future and will-future* — Seite 38–39

1 It's Friday afternoon. Sally, Max and Robin are talking about their plans for the weekend:
Sally: "What are you going to do tomorrow, Robin?" Robin: "I'm not sure, but I heard the weather forecast this morning. Tomorrow it won't rain. It will be a sunny day.
So I think I will go swimming"
Max: "Great idea, but I'm afraid I can't come. I've already packed my suitcase, because this weekend we are going to visit my aunt in Scotland. "

2 a) What are you going to do tomorrow? (Plan für die nähere Zukunft)
b) When are you going to do your homework? (Plan für die nähere Zukunft)
c) Who will help you/will somebody help you? (Liegt außerhalb der Planung des Sprechers)
d) Where are you going to work with him? (Plan für nähere Zukunft)

3 The Channel Tunnel

John Smith's Spanish friend, Manuel, is going to visit him in London. Marcel gets seasick easily, so he is afraid of traveling across the Channel. Ferries, hovercraft or catamarans were described to him as noisy and not very comfortable in stormy weather. Marcel can't afford to go by plane.
So he has decided on a train journey through the Channel Tunnel. Although the tickets are expensive, too, Marcel prefers the quiet trip under the English Channel through the 50-km-long railway tunnel.
He could not have chosen this route thirty years ago, when Britain and France were still separated by the sea and the island was cut off from the rest of Europe. But in 1994 miners successfully finished the huge project. Now the season for traveling is no longer restricted by weather conditions, and even people like Marcel can enjoy their journey and look forward to seeing the Crown Jewels, London pigeons and Piccadilly Circus.

Klassenarbeit Nr. 3 — Seite 40–41

Falls nicht anders angegeben, gibt es für jede Teilaufgabe bzw. jeden Teilschritt einen Punkt.

1 Susanne: We want to visit you in England. Are you home?
Sally: Yes, we are all home next week. You're welcome!
Susanne: Sie sagt, nächste Woche sind sie alle zu Hause und wir können kommen.
Sabine: Super. Frag doch mal, wie das Wetter werden soll.
Susanne: Great! What will the weather be like next week?
Sally: I've heard it will be cloudy and windy. Usually the weather isn't so nice here in May.
Susanne: Sie sagt, sie hat gehört es wird wolkig und windig. Meistens sei das Wetter im Mai bei ihnen nicht so schön.
Sabine: Kannst du sie fragen, ob man schon im Meer schwimmen kann?
Susanne: Sabine wants to know if the sea will be warm enough to swim in.
Sally: No, I suppose it will be too cold. Will Sabine come, too?
Susanne: Yes, she will. Sabine, sie sagt, dass es wohl noch zu kalt sein wird.
Sabine: Oh, sehr schade. Wird sie uns vom Bahnhof abholen?
Susanne: Sally, can you pick us up from the station?
Sally: Well, when does your train arrive at Dover?
Susanne: Sie will wissen, wann unser Zug ankommen wird.
Sabine: Das werden wir erst wissen, wenn wir am Bahnhof gefragt haben.
Susanne: Sabine says we will only know when we have asked at the station.
Sally: Don't arrive before twelve o'clock because nobody will be home unil then.
Susanne: Sie sagt wir sollen nicht vor Zwölf kommen, da ist noch keiner daheim.
Sabine: Alles Klar.

Ziehe dir für jeden Fehler einen Punkt ab.

2 a) What are you going to do at the weekend? I'm going to visit my aunt.
b) What will the weather be like on Monday? The weather won't be too nice on Monday.
c) How much money will we need (for the train ticket)? We will need about £20.

3 a) Tom: "I think, I will call Jane tomorrow."
b) Jane: "We are climbing/are going to climb in the mountains next weekend."
c) Her birthday is next Wednesday.
d) Jill: "We are going to fly to Chicago this summer. I've already bought the tickets."
e) On Monday I'm going to see the doctor.
f) It's rather cold. It 's going to snow soon.
g) Bond: "I have to hurry. The train leaves at half past two this afternoon."
h) John: "Don't worry. I will do the shopping for you."
i) The German team won't win a gold medal.

22–18 Punkte	17–11 Punkte	10–0 Punkte
Super!	In Ordnung!	Bitte noch einmal üben!

Kapitel 4: *Auxiliaries*

Test 1: *Auxiliaries do, have, be* — Seite 46–47

1 Libby and Anna <u>are</u> <u>doing</u> a project on Martin Waldseemüller for school.
They <u>have</u> already found out a lot about his life and work. They <u>are</u> planning to make a big poster which <u>has</u> all the important facts and figures. At the moment they <u>are</u> writing down some dates. After they <u>have</u> written down the text, they <u>are</u> going to glue some pictures of Waldseemüller and his famous map of America on the poster, too.
Before they <u>did</u> the written work, Libby and Anna <u>had</u> read a lot of books on the discovery of the New World, because they <u>had</u> not heard the name Waldseemüller before. But Anna's grandfather, who <u>has</u> always <u>been</u> very interested in history, gave

them some good advice on which books to read.

2 a) I don't do homework on Sundays.
Do als Vollverb nicht vergessen.
b) I'm going to do my homework tomorrow.
c) I will have done my homework by Friday.
d) I have been doing homework for two hours and I haven't finished yet.
Present prefect progressive wegen Signalwort *for two hours*: Eine Tätigkeit, die seit zwei Stunden ununterbrochen im Gange und zum Zeitpunkt des Sprechens noch nicht beendet ist.
e) I hadn't done my homework when the teacher asked me for it.
Keine *to-do*-Umschreibung im *past perfect*.

3 a) Every pupil must wear/has to wear a clean school uniform.
b) Pupils mustn't/are not allowed to/may not/can't wear jeans and sneakers/trainers in lesson.
c) Every pupil must be/has to be punctual.
d) Everybody should be/ought to be/must be treated with respect.
e) Nobody should disturb/ought to disturb the lessons.
f) Older pupils may/ are allowed to/can use the cafeteria.
g) Everybody should tidy up/ought to tidy up their own rubbish themselves.
h) Younger pupils may/are allowed to/can play football at break time.
i) After the lessons every pupil must put/has to put their chair on their table.
j) During the lessons everybody must/has to be quiet in school.
k) Pupils and teachers mustn't/are not allowed to/may not/can't smoke in school.

Test 2: *Modal auxiliaries* — Seite 48

1 a) Today I ☒ **can't** ☐ **am not able to** go to the youth club dance, because my Dad said no.
b) He said I **won't** ☐ **be able** ☒ **be allowed to** go out again unless I do better at school.
c) Tom ☐ **mustn't** ☒ **doesn't have to** work today.
d) He ☒ **is allowed to** ☐ **is able** to stay home.
e) You ☒ **may** ☐ **must** use my car today. I don't need it.
f) Yesterday Tom ☒ **couldn't** ☒ **wasn't able to** play football because he was injured.

2 a) I have been able to run a marathon.
b) You couldn't/weren't able to run a marathon.
c) You will have to leave now.
d) You should have done/ought to have done your homework.
e) Why did you have to see the doctor?
f) I will be able to see you tomorrow.
g) John has been allowed to visit you.
h) You were supposed to take the bus.
i) Jane had not been allowed to leave the house.
j) What will they be supposed to do for the project?

Klassenarbeit Nr. 4 — Seite 49–50

Falls nicht anders angegeben, gibt es für jede Teilaufgabe bzw. jeden Teilschritt einen Punkt.

1 a) I have been doing a project for school.
b) You will be late.
c) You didn't do your homework in time.
d) Mike is going to be a teacher.
e) I had had a great holiday job.
Je 2 Punkte

2 a) I have had to go to school by bike since September.
b) The bus ticket has become so expensive that I have not been able to afford it since then.
c) My father couldn't/wasn't able to take me in his car because he needed it himself.
d) My mother might buy a second car soon.
e) Then I will not need to/have to take the bus.
f) I hope I will be allowed to take her car often.
Je 2 Punkte

3 a) "Hi mum. Your new car looks great. It must have been very expensive."
b) "No, it was a special offer. I could not/was not able to/would not buy an expensive car."
c) "Am I allowed to/Can/May I use it, too?"
d) "You can/may/are allowed to use it but you must/should always ask me first."
e) "And I might need it myself most of the time."

4 James Bond has just returned from a mission and is talking to his boss M.
M: "How did you get back without your car?"
Bond: "I simply had to walk. There was no other way."
M: " Could/Were you able to finish your mission?"
Bond: "Of course, Sir. I could/was able to steal the CD you wanted. Here it is.

By the way, can I see my new car? "
M: "No, I'm afraid not. Q has to do some other work first. But yesterday he showed me some of the new weapons for your car."
Bond: "Really? I wasn't allowed to see them. He told me to come back later. I hope I will be able to handle the new car by next weekend."
M: "I hope so, too. That's another very important mission for you. We can't risk a failure"

37–30 Punkte	29–19 Punkte	18–0 Punkte
Super!	In Ordnung!	Bitte noch einmal üben!

Kapitel 5: *Conditional sentences*

Test 1: *First conditional* — Seite 53

1

If you join a club,	if he always eats lots of sweets.
I'll have the rest of the weekend free,	if they go on holiday to London.
If we watch a horror film in the dark,	if I do all my homework on Friday.
If she wins the modelling competition,	you'll meet lots of new friends.
They'll probably visit the London Eye,	we'll get scared.
All his teeth will fall out,	a magazine will definitely offer her a contract.

2 Possible answers.
a) If you play violent computer games, you will become more aggressive.
b) Your hair will fall out if you dye it constantly.
c) If you come home late, your parents will be annoyed.
d) The teacher will get angry if we talk during his lesson.
e) If you spend all your money on clothes, you won't be able to buy CDs or snacks.
f) If you don't install an internet firewall, viruses will attack your computer.

In dem Teil des Satzes, der *if* enthält, wird das *simple present*, im anderen Teil des Satzes wird *will-future* benutzt.

3 a) If you are hungry, my mum/mother will cook something for you.
b) If you are scared of dogs, I will leave our rottweiler in the garden.
c) The neighbours will complain, if we play music too loudly.

Test 2: *Second conditional* — Seite 54–55

1 a) My dad gave me this ring. He would be upset if I lost it.
b) If you didn't pass the exams, would you repeat the school year?
c) How would he get home if the busses were cancelled?
d) My bike is very old, I wouldn't get much money, if I sold it.
e) Would you lend him money if he asked you?

In dem Teil des Satzes, der *if* enthält, wird das *simple past*, im anderen Teil des Satzes wird *would* benutzt.

2 Linda: "Shall we take the 7:00 bus?
Jack: "No, if we took it, we would arrive too early."
Linda: "Why don't we follow my elder brother too the disco?"
Jack: "If we followed him, we would get into trouble."
Linda: "How shall we get home, by bus or by taxi?"
Jack: "If we got home by taxi, it would be expensive.
Linda: "Shall I ask Laura out from class 8A?"
Jack: "No, if she said no, it would be rather embarrassing."
Linda: "Do you think I should wear a skirt or jeans to the party? "
Jack: "Jeans. If you wore a skirt, you could get quite cold."

3 a) If you joined a club, you would/could meet a lot of new friends.
b) If you didn't buy so many DVDs, you would have more money left at the end of the month.
c) If you didn't wear a skirt, you wouldn't feel so cold.
d) If you had saved more money, you could buy a new computer.

Klassenarbeit Nr. 5 — Seite 56–58

Falls nicht anders angegeben, gibt es für jede Teilaufgabe bzw. jeden Teilschritt einen Punkt.

1 a) I would fix your bike if I had a screwdriver of the correct size, but I don't.
Second conditional – möglich aber unwahrscheinlich. Es steht im ersten Teil schon *would*, also brauchst du *simple past* im zweiten Teil.
b) I will make a salad for the picnic, if the tomatoes in my garden are ripe.
First conditional – möglich und wahrscheinlich. Es steht im zweiten Teil

schon *simple present*, also im ersten Teil brauchst du *will-future*.

c) If you don't do more sport, you won't feel fitter.
First conditional – Warnung vor den Folgen des Handelns.

d) If they lived closer, they would see each other more often.
Second conditional – Wünsche ausdrücken.

e) What would he say, if he knew you broke his computer?
Second conditional – unwahrscheinlich, aber möglich.

f) If the house were ever on fire, we could escape through the window.
Second conditional – unwahrscheinlich, aber möglich

Pro Verbform 1 Punkt, gesamt 10 Punkte

2 Hi! How are you? What have you been doing recently? I ~~go~~ went to a party yesterday and met some boys. We were dancing, and one kissed my friend Lizzie. Then they ~~had~~ offered us vodka and the boy and Lizzie went outside. I wonder what they ~~have done~~ did. There's another party this weekend, but shall I go? One guy is very attractive, but how can I tell if he likes me? If I drank vodka and ~~wear~~ wore a skirt, I would look cool. But I ~~was not~~ wouldn't be happy with drinking vodka. I don't think it's good to drink alcohol and then kiss boys, but if I warned Lizzie, she ~~will~~ would think I'm annoying. What can I do? Write soon! Sarah

1 Punkt für jeden richtig entdeckten Fehler, noch 1 Punkt für jede richtige Korrektur – Gesamt 12 Punkte

3 a) False: If you travel east from Wales, you will be in England. 2 Punkte

b) False: If you are in Wales on 1st March, you will see people eating Welsh rarebit (cheese on toast). 2 Punkte

c) True: 1 Punkt

d) False: If you see signs for *Cardiff*, you are in the south of Wales. 2 Punkte

e) True: 2 Punkte

4 a) Since the 600s (5th century), Wales has had its own history of literature.

b) Since the 1800s, Wales has had a thriving industry in coal and steel.

c) In the 1980s, the Conservative government closed down lots of factories and mines.

d) In 1955, Cardiff became the Wales' capital city.

e) In 1999, Wales opened its own small parliament, called the "National Assembly."

Je 2 Punkte

5 a) Model answers
Deine Sätze müssen im *Second Conditional* geschrieben werden, da es sich um eine unwahrscheinliche Situation handelt.
Pro Satz 2 Punkte: 1 Punkt für den *if*-Teil, 1 Punkt für den anderen Teil, wenn Verbform korrekt
If I had £1000 to spend, I would buy lots of new clothes. I would also buy some new CDs if I had £1000. If I had £1000, I would throw a big party. If I threw a big party, I would wear my new clothes and play my new CDs. It would be fun if all my friends came. If too many people came, I would lock the door.

b) Model answers
Deine Sätze sollen im *Second Conditional* geschrieben werden, da es sich um eine unwahrscheinliche Situation handelt.
Pro Satz 2 Punkte: 1 Punkt für den if-Teil, 1 Punkt für den anderen Teil, wenn Verbform korrekt.
If I were 70 years old, I would visit my grandchildren in my free time. If I had a husband, he would play golf and I would watch him. I would go to the theatre if I were 70 years old, because I would have a lot of free time. I would also read a lot of books if I was/were retired and didn't have to write essays about them!

56–46 Punkte	45–28 Punkte	27–0 Punkte
Super!	In Ordnung!	Bitte noch einmal üben!

Klassenarbeit Nr. 6 — Seite 59–60

Falls nicht anders angegeben, gibt es für jede Teilaufgabe bzw. jeden Teilschritt einen Punkt.

1 a) If you don't understand something, I'll translate it for you.

b) If you had your MP3-Player with you, we could exchange music.

c) You will get to know my boyfriend if we go to the disco.

d) If you don't put slippers on, your feet will get cold.

e) If my mother wasn't so strict, we wouldn't have to go to bed so early.

Jeweils 2 Punkte: 1 Punkt für den *if*-Teil, 1 Punkt für den anderen Teil, wenn Verbform korrekt

2 Model answers

a) If you train with weights/do weightlifting, you will become strong/muscly.

b) If you eat pizza every day, you will get fat.

c) You will cough (a lot) if you smoke.

d) If you run fast, you will win the cup/a prize.

Pro Satz 2 Punkte: 1 Punkt für den *if*-Teil, 1 Punkt für den anderen Teil, wenn Verbform korrekt

3 a) 87 girls from a Catholic sixth-form college.

b) Whether watching music videos with slim/sexily-dressed girl bands makes girls feel bad about their bodies.

c) Girls who watch music videos feel less happy about their bodies than those who just hear the music or read word lists.

Je 2 Punkte

4

	true	false	not in the text
a)	☐	☒	☐
b)	☒	☐	☐
c)	☐	☒	☐
d)	☐	☐	☒
e)	☒	☐	☐

5 Model answers

Deine Sätze sollen einen Teil mit *if + simple past*, und einen Teil mit *would* enthalten.

If I could pick any country, I would travel to France. If I travelled to France, I would get there by train. If I went by train, it wouldn't take very long.

Pro Satz 1 Punkt für den *if*-Teil, 1 Punkt für den anderen Teil, wenn Verbform korrekt

6 Model answers

If he/she weren't so loud, she wouldn't be so unlikeable./If you bring him/her to the party next week, we will all be annoyed./If you continue to date him/her, you will lose a lot of friends.

Pro Satz 1 Punkt für den *if*-Teil, 1 Punkt für den anderen Teil, wenn Verbform korrekt

44–36 Punkte	35–22 Punkte	21–0 Punkte
Super!	In Ordnung!	Bitte noch einmal üben!

Kapitel 6: *Passive voice*

Test 1: Passiv (I) — Seite 64

1

story	Title for the newspaper article
Thieves stole £1000 from a bank yesterday.	£1000 was stolen from a bank yesterday
The band has cancelled all the concerts in May.	All the concerts in May have been cancelled by the band
Someone took photos of the celebrities' secret wedding.	Photos of the celebrities' secret wedding were taken
The Queen will visit children in hospital.	Children in hospital will be visited by the Queen
Somone is constantly watching the prisoners in the new jail.	The prisoners in the new jail are constantly being watched
Shakespeare copied *Macbeth* from another author!	*Macbeth* was copied from another author by Shakespeare
Paparazzi were chasing Diana when she was killed.	Diana was being chased by paparazzi when she was killed

2 One of the most famous catastrophes in history happened on April 2, 1912 when the luxury liner „RMS Titanic" hit an iceberg and was slashed open. The problem was that the iceberg was spotted too late by lookout Frederick Fleet so that the collision couldn't be avoided. Soon five of the ship's watertight compartments were flooded. Passengers and some crew members were evacuated in lifeboats. But because the crew wasn't trained adequately for such a disaster, many of the lifeboats were only partly filled. Most of the men were left on board because women and children had to be rescued first. Two hours and forty minutes after the collision the ship broke into two halves and the people onboard were thrown into the icecold water. Almost all of them died within minutes. When the „Titanic" sank a number of distress signals were sent but no other ship was near enough to arrive in time. In the end about 1500 people were killed and only 710 could be rescued.

Test 2: Passiv (II) — Seite 65–67

1

The punctured tyres,	take care of your bike.
You must always	was fitted to the handle bars and polished.
My brother	were repaired by my brother.
A new bell	had to be oiled.
Several hours	helped me a lot.
The bike chain	were needed to complete all the jobs.

2 a) I have recently been named gymnast of the year at my school.
b) Last year, the under-21s world championship was won by my team.
c) A famous sports shop sponsors my kit.
d) Is the equipment checked the equipment regularly by experts?
e) I understand that the equipment must be put away by the athletes.

3 a) Yes, I have been given a report about the destroyed sports centre./Yes, a report about the destroyed sports centre has been given to me.
b) No, they were not offered financial help by the insurance company./ No, financial help was not offered to them by the insurance company.
c) Yes, they will be given money to rebuild the sports centre./Yes, money will be given to them to rebuild the sports centre.
d) Yes, the children have been promised new equipment./Yes, new equipment has been promised to the children.
e) Yes, a sports celebrity will be sent to the centre to open the new play areas./Yes, the centre will be sent a sports celebrity to open the new play areas.

4

to take advantage of	auf etwas stolz sein
to make friends with	verwenden
to make use of	ausnutzen
to pay attention to	aus dem Auge verlieren
to lose track of	auf etwas achten
to take pride in	sich mit jemandem anfreunden

5 a) The old factory was blown up.
b) The dog's short tail was being made fun of.
c) The broken fence was taken advantage of.

Klassenarbeit Nr. 7 — Seite 67–70

Falls nicht anders angegeben, gibt es für jede Teilaufgabe bzw. jeden Teilschritt einen Punkt.

1 a) NASA: National Aeronatics and Space Administration.
SETI: Search for Extraterrestrial Intelligence.
b) 1958: NASA was founded and American space exploration was started.
1996: Meteorites from Mars were studied by scientists and evidence of life on Mars from billions of years ago was found.
1997: Mars was reached by Mars Pathfinder and Mars Global Surveyor (NASA spaceships).
2000: Life was found in the icy waters of Jupiter's moons by Galileo (NASA shuttle).

2 a) For ~~four~~ years, scientists have been trying to find life on other planets.
For years 2 Punkte
b) Water and a suitable temperature may be signs of life on a planet. ✓ 1 Punkt
c) ~~People lived~~ on Mars billions of years ago. There are signs of life 2 Punkte
d) Scientists ~~listen to the radio~~ to finds signs of extraterrestrial life. Scientists use radio telescopes 2 Punkte
e) Scientists have found a star and group of planets similar to our solar system. ✓
1 Punkte

3 a) The Explorer I satellite was sent into orbit by NASA.
b) The ground and rocks on Mars will be studies by astronauts.
c) The planet Mars has been taken pictures of by spacecraft.
d) Life in other worlds is being looked for by another programme.
Pro Satz 2 Punkte, 1 für Verbform, wenn richtig, 1 für richtigen Satzbau

4 a) When were computers invented?
b) Who were computers invented by?
c) How are computers made?
d) Where are the most computers sold?
e) What are computers used for?
f) Is a new computer being developed?
Pro Satz 2 Punkte, 1 für Verbform, wenn richtig, 1 für richtigen Satzbau

5 At the moment my parents are building [active voice] a new house near the river. About one year ago, they went [active voice] to the bank and were given [passive voice, weil das Geld den Eltern gegeben wird, wer es gegeben hat, ist nicht offensichtlich.] some money to pay for the new house.

The bank agreed [active voice] to lend £150,000, but £50,000 had to be provided [passive voice, in der Vergangenheit – "£50,000" ist wichtig und wird betont] by mum and dad. The building work started [active voice] last January and the whole house will be finished [passive voice Futur, das Haus ist wichtig und wird betont, wer baut ist unwichtig/nicht gewusst] next month. Then the inside will have to be decorated [passive voice, weil wer das tut, ist nicht wichtig, Achtung: Umschreibung von "Must" → "to have to" um Futur Passiv zu bilden]. I will paint [active voice] my room blue, but my sister's room will be painted [passive voice, weil wer das tut nicht bekannt ist] in pink. We will all be [active voice in future, weil "happy" ein Adjektiv ist und kein Partizip II] happy when we have moved in [active voice] to our new house.

6

planet	Mars	Mercury	Neptune
highest temperature	20 °C	427 °C	
lowest temperature	–140 °C	–173°C	–218°C
time taken to orbit sun	687 days	Quicker than Earth	165 years
size	Second smallest		17 x Earth

7 a) We know Mars as the *red planet*/ Another name for Mars is the *red planet*.
b) Ice covers the north and south poles of Mars.
c) Gas makes up the planet Neptune.
d) ...since people/scientists/astronomers discovered Neptune in 1846.

2 Punkte für jeden Satz: 1 für richtige Zeitform von *to be*, 1 für richtiges Partizip II

8 Individuelle Lösung.
Deine Geschichte soll möglichst viele Passivsätze und verschiedene Zeitformen beinhalten.
Ziehe dir für jeden Fehler einen Punkt ab. Vielleicht findest du jemanden, der die Korrektur für dich erledigt?

78–67 Punkte	66–39 Punkte	38–0 Punkte
Super!	In Ordnung!	Bitte noch einmal üben!

Klassenarbeit Nr. 8 — Seite 71–74

Falls nicht anders angegeben, gibt es für jede Teilaufgabe bzw. jeden Teilschritt einen Punkt.

1 a) Die Fußballtrikots müssen jede Woche gewaschen werden.
b) The playing fields may only be used by children.
c) Fußball konnte nur zwischen 8 Uhr und 21 Uhr gespielt werden. [Achtung: hier ist could die Vergangenheitsform von can, nicht Konjunktiv!]
d) If possible, the terrible food in the canteen should be avoided!
e) Die Finale hätten verschoben werden können, weil das Wetter so schlecht war.

Pro Antwort 2 Punkte: 1 für richtige Passivkonstruktion, 1 für den Rest des Satzes

2 a) No, the books will be given to the next class pupils at the end of the year, not to another school!
b) No, we will be asked normal questions in the test, not tricky questions!
c) No, I was sent a funny email by Lucy yesterday, not an SMS!
d) No, I have been told a story about the witch, not the ghost!
e) No, a sponsorship contract has been offered to the hockey team by Nike, not to the football team!
f) No, she was promised a lot of money by her mother if she gets good grades, not sweets! Je 2 Punkte

3 a) The new band was/were being talked about all day.
b) All the glasses had been washed up.
c) The road signs have not been paid attention to.

Pro Antwort 2 Punkte: 1 für richtige Passivkonstruktion, 1 für den Rest des Satzes

4 Model answers
a) Dolphins often swim near tuna fish and when fishermen fish to catch the tuna, the dolphins are caught up in the fishing nets and are often killed.
b) *Dolphin friendly* products are made using fish that was caught using fishing methods or nets that do not hurt dolphins.
c) *Whale and Dolphin Conservation Society*, charity that wants to improve the lives and protection of whales and dolphins. They want to raise awareness of the threats to the mammals and their habitats to make sure they do not die out.

2 Punkte pro Anwort, für richtige Grammatik und Informationen

5

	true	false	not in the text
a)	☐	☒	☐
b)	☐	☒	☐
c)	☒	☐	☐
d)	☐	☒	☐
e)	☐	☒	☐
f)	☐	☐	☒
g)	☒	☐	☐

6 a) conservation b) alongside
c) harm d) entirely
e) raise f) improve
Hier brauchst du nur drei Richtige, da die Aufgabe schwer ist, weil die Wörter nicht zum „normalen" Wortschatz gehören.

7 Fish 'n' chips (was once called) "the most British dinner". But how is it made? Well, the fresh fish is covered in batter and deep fried in oil. After the raw potatoes have been cut, they are boiled and fried as chips.
British chips are much thicker than American fries. When everything is ready, the fish is served together with the chips. Sometimes it is accompanied by mushy peas or sprinkled with salt and vinegar, but this has gone out of fashion recently. In the past, fish 'n' chips (was wrapped) in paper and (eaten) with a small wooden fork. Traditionally the meal (was enjoyed) on a Friday evening, though tourists don't follow this rule!
1 Punkt pro richtige Markierung, maximal 8 Punkte

8 Individuelle Lösung.
Lass jemanden korrigieren, der in Englisch fit ist. Vielleicht hat auch deine Englischlehrkraft Zeit.

9 Individuelle Lösung.
Lass jemanden korrigieren, der in Englisch fit ist. Vielleicht hat auch deine Englischlehrkraft Zeit.

76–62 Punkte	61–38 Punkte	37–0 Punkte
Super!	In Ordnung!	Bitte noch einmal üben!

Kapitel 7: *Pronouns and determiners*

Test 1: *Personal and possessive pronouns* Seite 79–80

1 John Smith is a new boy in form 7c.
He has got a lot of questions. Sue and Linda, some girls from his new form, are showing him all the important places on the school grounds. "We have got a few clubs in our school," says Sue. "This is where the stamp club meets every Thursday. Are you interested in books? Mrs Gordon's literature club is very popular. She is our English teacher, I think you've already met her." "And here are the sports facilities. I am a member of the girls hockey team, but a lot of boys play hockey, too. They practise every Monday afternoon." "Can you tell me if there is a soccer team, too?" "Oh, you should ask Mr Piller, the sport teacher. If you want to know anything about football, just ask him." "We must go now. Mum is meeting us in town in ten minutes. But look, Jack and Robert are over there. If you have got any more questions, ask them. I'm sure they will help you."

2 The Miller family lives near my/our house. There are five of them. Their names are Paul, Mary, Sue, Linda and Frank. Frank Miller is the youngest member. Sue and Linda are his sisters. Sue and Linda are twins. Frank is their brother, of course. What's the name of the mother? Her name is Mary. Linda: "And our father is called Paul."

3 Mrs Miller: Look at this t-shirt. Is it yours, Linda?
Sue: No, it's not. It's mine. Linda always takes my things without asking me.
Mrs Miller: And these shoes, are they yours, too?
Sue: No, they aren't, they are hers.
Mrs Miller: Are these Linda's CDs or yours?
Sue: Oh, these aren't ours at all. We must give them back to John, they are his.
Mrs Miller: And these earrings, I think I have seen them before …
Sue: Sorry, Mum, they are yours.
Mrs Miller: Sue, if you take your sister's things, that is your/her business, but I want you to ask me before you take my things.

4 a) Linda and Sue got many presents for their birthday.
b) Linda gave her sister Sue a CD.
c) Sue gave Linda her favourite book.
d) Linda and Sue always give each other a present for their birthday.
e) They put all their presents on a big table.
f) Many friends came to visit them and gave them presents.

Test 2: *Reflexive pronouns* Seite 81

1 a) Sue and Linda are old enough to look after themselves.
b) John is introducing himself to form 7c.
c) We are enjoying ourselves at the party.

d) Help yourselves to ice cream, girls. I bought all your favourite flavours.
e) My mother never buys ice cream. She makes it herself.
f) Frank, stop fooling around and behave yourself in class.
g) Look at my thumb. I cut myself when chopping onions yesterday.

2 a) The door opened itself. It must have been the wind.
b) I don't remember having ever seen such a storm before.
c) Not many people enjoy themselves in such weather.
d) Many old people don't feel well when the weather changes so quickly.
e) My grandma always talks to herself then to stay calm.

3 a) herself
b) each other
c) yourself
d) each other/one another
e) each other/one another
f) herself

Test 3: *Relative pronouns* Seite 82

1 a) Everybody in our school has heard about the boy whose mobile phone was confiscated last Monday.
b) The boy who/that has got twin sisters is called Frank Miller.
c) The boy whose twin sisters are called Sue and Linda is in my form.
d) The bell whose sound could be heard in class is Big Ben.
e) The mobile phone which/that disrupted class with the sound of Big Ben belongs to Frank Miller.
f) The mobile phone whose sound disrupted class was confiscated by the headmaster.
g) I need a mobile phone which doesn't make a sound at all.
h) The parents whose son got into trouble had to talk to the headmaster.
i) The discussion which/that lasted about ten minutes was not very pleasant.
j) The headmaster is a man who/that always insists on keeping the school rules.

2 a) This is Aunt Jessica, whose family emigrated to Australia 200 years ago.
b) This is Uncle Robert, who married Aunt Jessica twenty years ago.
c) This is a part of the Australian outback which has some very dangerous snakes.
d) This is a beautiful house which they bought for their children.
e) This is my first boyfriend, whose name was Sean.

Klassenarbeit Nr. 9 Seite 83–85

Falls nicht anders angegeben, gibt es für jede Teilaufgabe bzw. jeden Teilschritt einen Punkt.

1 a) To protect the environment you/one should use your/one's bike more often.
b) You know that riding a bike is good for you.
c) If you use your car less, you also save money.
Je 2 Punkte

2 a) Sue and Linda talk to each other/one another about everything.
b) They know each other/one another like nobody else.
c) Sue and Linda are looking at themselves in the bathroom mirror.
d) The sisters help each other/one another with their hair styles.
e) They always talk to each other/one another before they get a new haircut.
f) But they never do these haircuts themselves.

3 a) Is John Miller the pupil who got into trouble last Monday?
b) Here is his mobile phone whose sound disrupted class.
c) These are our school rules which/that say mobile phones mustn't be used in class.
d) The teacher who/that took John's mobile phone away is Mr Finch, John's form teacher.
e) Mr Gill, who is the headmaster, is very angry. (oder: Mr Gill, who is very angry, is the headmaster.)
Je 2 Punkte

4 a) "I can take care of myself, Mum," Linda said as she went on the bus to Devon.
b) "Well, enjoy yourself and call us when you arrive," Linda's mother answered.
c) "I will, Mum, John, Sue and I will certainly enjoy ourselves at the festival, it's always great fun!"
d) On the bus Linda and Sue were so excited they started singing to themselves/each other.
e) John and the girls met in Exeter. They kissed each other and then John said: "I've booked us the same lovely rooms in the hostel we had last year. We are really lucky this year!"

f) When they got to the hostel, Linda didn't remember the bump in the stairs and hurt herself when she stumbled and fell.
g) But it wasn't too bad and some time later she was able to move again and laugh about herself.

5 a) John and Jenny were very surprised when they met (one another) on the train to the festival.
b) They saw each other through the window of the compartment and smiled at each other.
c) Jenny's boyfriend saw them through the window from outside when they were sitting next to each other.
d) He was angry at himself because he himself couldn't come to the festival.

Je 2 Punkte

6 **A Man of Many Wives**

Henry VIII was King of England from 1509 until his death. Henry VIII was the second son of Henry VII and Elizabeth of York and only became king because their elder son Arthur died in 1502. Henry VIII is well-known because he was married to six different women: Catherine of Aragon, Anne Boleyn, Jane Seymor, Anne of Cleves, Katherine Howard, and Catherine Parr. During his reign as king many important laws were made. Henry named himself as supreme Head of the Church of England, and used his new position to get divorced from his first wife, Catherine of Aragon. The lives of his six wives can be summarized as follows: divorced, beheaded, died, divorced, beheaded, survived. Catherine Parr survived, as her husband died before she did. Anne of Cleves also outlived him, after their divorce. Three of his six wives bore Henry children who survived their childhood and all of them ruled England: Edward VI, Mary I and Elizabeth I.

53–45 Punkte	44–27 Punkte	26–0 Punkte
Super!	In Ordnung!	Bitte noch einmal üben!

Kapitel 8: *Adverb and adjective*

Test 1: *Adjective and adverb: Form*

Seite 90

1 a) Linda and Sue are twins, but Linda is prettier than Sue.
Yes, but Sue is the cleverer of the two.
b) I got the best mark in today's test. But it was the easiest test we have had this year. Last week's test was much more difficult.
c) Can I have more champagne, please?
No, you can't. You have had the most already.
That is not true. I have had less than you.
d) Which is the biggest town in Europe? I don't know, but Munich is certainly the most interesting and safer than most other big towns in the world.
e) Our new form teacher is much nicer than our old one. Yes, but the old one was one of the strictest teachers I have ever met.

2 a) slowly
b) easily
c) fast
d) carefully
e) hard
f) badly
g) terribly
h) unfortunately
i) higly
j) well

3 a) A Mercedes is not as elegant as a Rolls Royce.
b) Yes, but a Rolls Royce is also much more expensive than a Mercedes.
c) The fastest and most beautiful cars are made by Porsche.
d) A Ford is not as fast, but it is also much cheaper.
e) My car is the worst you can have.

Test 2: *Adjective and adverb: Use*

Seite 91–92

1 Linda has to do her homework again because it was done badly. Sue didn't have to do hers again because she did it ever so carefully. But Linda had done her homework very fast because she doesn't like to work hard. Now she is sitting in her room quietly, writing beautifully in her best handwriting. She knows that this time she must work well or her teacher will shout at her angrily tomorrow. Linda thinks she is not treated fair because Sue always gets on easily with all her teachers because she can be extremely polite.

2 Linda's exercise book is full of mistakes – extremely full, it has never been as bad as this year. Most of these mistakes happen because Linda is not doing her work carefully. Her head is always in the clouds and what she likes best is dreaming about her lovely boyfriend John. Her sister Sue is very angry with Linda because she hates being told off by the teacher – especially since Sue always does her homework ever so carefully. But Mrs Brown sometimes still confuses the

twins and then Sue doesn't think it is funny to be punished for what her lazy sister does wrong.

3 a) "Why are you so sad Linda?"
b) "I think Miss Brown has really treated me badly"
c) "Why, what terrible things did she do?"
d) "Well, usually she is very nice, but yesterday she made me feel uncomfortable because of my homework."
e) "What was wrong with it?"
f) "I had done it quite hastily because I came home hungry and she said I was just too lazy to care about my work."

4 a) Linda sings well.
b) Sue listens carefully.
c) John plays football badly.
d) I drive fast.
e) We play fair.

5 a) Linda always works at the weekend.
b) She never gets home before six in the evening.
c) Linda and Sue often go to the cinema.
d) Linda is very tired. She hardly sleeps enough.
e) She has only/only has one free day per week.

6 **Los Angeles**
Manuel's cousin Ray moved to L.A. a few months ago because his uncle Diego had found a job as an accountant. They're typical immigrants who still speak Spanish at home. With a population of about 3.5 million, Los Angeles is the nation's second largest city. For some it means Hollywood and sunny weather, for others simply heavy traffic, air pollution, street gangs, ethnic problems and rough neighbourhoods.
Ray had just expected a beautiful climate and beaches, but there were many more interesting sights there to be seen, e.g. Disneyland or the mission area, where European priests once had tried to educate the Indians and turn them into Christians. Later Ray found out that California has different countrysides, large national parks, wild rivers and huge forests, too, and that you can go cycling in summer temperatures, relax and cool down by swimming or going skiing – all on the same day.

Klassenarbeit Nr. 10 — Seite 93–94

Falls nicht anders angegeben, gibt es für jede Teilaufgabe bzw. jeden Teilschritt einen Punkt.

1 For many people Wales is closely connected to Rugby because it is a very popular game there. In 1999 the Rugby World Cup Final Tournament was held in Cardiff's National Stadium, attracting fans from all over the world. The first Rugby World Cup Tournament was in 1987 and is repeated every four years. Rugby is thought to have originated when a boy at Rugby School in England picked up and carried the ball carefully during a game of football in 1823. Then the game of rugby became quite popular in other English schools and even today it is often the most popular game among male students.
Satzadverbien: Then
Adverbien der unbestitmmten Zeit/Häufigkeit: often
Modaladverbien: carefully
Lokaladverbien: there, in Cardiff's National Stadium, from all over the world, in England, in other English schools
Temporaladverbien: In 1999, in 1987, every four years, in 1823, even today
Gradadverbien: closely, very, quite

2 Complete the table with the missing forms.

adjective	Adverb	comparative	superlative
good	well	better	best
much	much	more	most
fast	fast	faster	fastest
big	big	bigger	biggest
loud	loudly	louder	loudest
funny	funnily	funnier	funniest
near	near	nearer	nearest
little	little	less	least
useful	usefully	more useful	most useful
terrible	terribly	more terrible	most terrible

3 There is no better country for a bike tour than Wales. You can easliy keep away from big roads and enjoy the beautiful landscape. There are many lanes with few cars. It's really a cyclist's paradise! Of course there are not only famous national parks like Snowdonia, Pembrokeshire Coast, and Brecon Beacons which are always perfect for a bike tour, but often the normal places with their beautiful scenery are attractive. Maybe you see not only rivers, but beavers, salmon and other wildlife animals often appear here.

4 All about Wales

Wales is situated in the sunny south-west of Great Britain.
To the west and north of Wales is the Irish Sea and ferries run regularly across to Cork from Swansea, which is Wales' second-largest city.
Since the 1800s Wales has been a successful industrial state and still exports a lot of coal and steel.
However, many factories and mines were closed down in the 1980s and the service industry became more successful.
Most of the Welsh population lives quietly in the valleys and the coastal areas of South Wales.
Other areas, in Mid Wales, the south west and west are mainly hilly countryside areas.
The capital city of Wales, Cardiff, is also in the south. In this area English is the most commonly used language, although a separate Welsh language exists and all official documents and road-signs are bilingual.
A separate parliament for Wales, the "National Assembly", was formed in 1999, and has limited power to pass laws independent of the main U.K. Parliament in London.
The Welsh people like to preserve their cultural identity. They wear traditional dress and eat traditional foods, such as Welsh cakes, rye bread, faggots, Welsh rarebit (cheese on toast) and corned-beef pasties.
Wales is also famous for choirs, sheep, rugby, whisky and mountain trekking, it is a good destination for your family holiday!

83–67 Punkte	66–41 Punkte	40–0 Punkte
Super!	In Ordnung!	Bitte noch einmal üben!

Stichwortregister